easy
summer food

easy summer food

simple recipes for sunny days

RYLAND
PETERS
& SMALL

LONDON NEW YORK

Designer Sarah Fraser

Commissioning Editor Elsa Petersen-Schepelern

Editor Sharon Cochrane

Production Gavin Bradshaw

Art Director Gabriella Le Grazie

Publishing Director Alison Starling

Index Hilary Bird

First published in Great Britain in 2005
by Ryland Peters & Small
20–21 Jockey's Fields
London WC1R 4BW
www.rylandpeters.com

10 9 8 7 6 5 4 3 2 1

Text © Julz Beresford, Maxine Clark, Clare Ferguson,
Elsa Petersen-Schepelern, Louise Pickford, Fran Warde,
Lesley Waters and Ryland Peters & Small 2005

Design and photographs © Ryland Peters & Small 2005

ISBN 1 84172 823 3

A CIP catalogue record for this book is available from
the British Library.

Printed in China

Notes

All spoon measurements are level unless otherwise
specified.

All eggs are medium unless otherwise specified.
Uncooked or partly cooked eggs should not be served
to the very young, the very old, those with compromised
immune systems or to pregnant women.

Ovens should be preheated to the specified temperature.
If using a fan-assisted oven, cooking times should be
reduced according to the manufacturer's instructions.

Specialist Asian ingredients are available in larger
supermarkets and Asian stores.

To sterilize preserving jars, wash them in hot, soapy
water and rinse in boiling water. Place in a large
saucepan and then cover with hot water. With the
saucepan lid on, bring the water to the boil and continue
boiling for 15 minutes. Turn off the heat, then leave the
jars in the hot water until just before they are to be
filled. Drain and dry. Sterilize the lids for 5 minutes, by
boiling, or according to the manufacturer's instructions.
Jars should be filled and sealed while they are still hot.

contents

a taste of summer

Summer is about enjoying the outdoors and relaxing over good food with good company. Crisp salad leaves, a handful of fresh berries, a scoop of ice cream, a cooling cocktail … these are the tastes of summer. This collection of recipes takes the best of the summer bounty and creates simple recipes to inspire you to make the most of what this fabulous season has to offer.

Covering everything from starters and main courses to sweet treats and cooling drinks, these easy recipes are all you need to enjoy summer to the full, whatever the occasion. Whether you are looking for a quick lunch for one, a stylish dinner for friends or just something to cool and refresh, this book is packed with easy ideas. Eating outdoors is one of the pleasures of summer and with lots of recipes for picnics and barbecues, **Easy Summer Food** will encourage you to get out of the house and into the garden, the park, the beach or wherever the sunshine happens to take you.

So, kick off your shoes, relax and enjoy a delicious summer with this great selection of easy sunshine food.

starters

Gazpacho is a light summer soup. It originated in the south of Spain, traditionally in Andalusia. For best results use ripe tomatoes and a good-quality olive oil – but, most importantly, serve it icy cold.

gazpacho

Grind the garlic and a pinch of salt together using a mortar and pestle.

Put the bread in a saucer with a little water and let soak. Put the garlic, bread, tomatoes, onion, cucumber and vinegar in a blender and purée until smooth. Keeping the motor running, add the oil in a slow and steady stream. Add salt and pepper to taste, then add the sugar.

Pour the mixture through a sieve into a bowl, adding more salt, pepper and vinegar if necessary. Cover and chill in the refrigerator overnight. Serve in small bowls or glasses with a little chopped cucumber sprinkled on top.

1 garlic clove

1 slice white bread, crusts removed

4 ripe juicy tomatoes, skinned and deseeded

1 tablespoon grated onion

¼ small cucumber, peeled and deseeded, plus extra to serve

1 tablespoon Spanish red wine vinegar

2 tablespoons olive oil

1 teaspoon sugar

sea salt and freshly ground black pepper

serves 4

On a hot summer's day a chilled soup is the perfect starter or lunch dish. This coconut soup is based on an original Thai recipe – the contrast with the hot, aromatic garlic prawns is just magical.

chilled coconut soup
with sizzling prawns

500 ml coconut milk

300 ml plain yoghurt

1 cucumber, peeled and chopped

2 tablespoons chopped fresh mint leaves

2 tablespoons extra virgin olive oil

2 garlic cloves, thinly sliced

½ teaspoon cumin seeds

a pinch of dried red chilli flakes

8–12 uncooked tiger prawns, peeled and deveined

sea salt and freshly ground black pepper

serves 4

Put the coconut milk, yoghurt, cucumber and mint in a blender or food processor and blend to a purée. Add salt and pepper to taste. Chill for 1 hour.

Ladle the soup into 4 bowls just before starting to cook the prawns.

Put the oil in a large frying pan and heat gently. Add the garlic, cumin seeds and chilli flakes and fry very gently until the garlic is softened, but not golden. Using a slotted spoon, transfer the garlic mixture to a small plate.

Increase the heat under the frying pan and add the prawns. Stir-fry for 3–4 minutes until cooked through. Return the garlic mixture to the pan, stir quickly, then immediately spoon the sizzling hot prawns onto the soup and serve.

pappa al pomodoro

*1 kg ripe red tomatoes, preferably
on the vine, chopped*

300 ml vegetable stock

1 teaspoon caster sugar

6 tablespoons extra virgin olive oil

4 sprigs of oregano

4 sprigs of basil

*125 g day-old bread,
crusts removed*

2 garlic cloves, halved

*sea salt and freshly ground
black pepper*

*freshly grated Parmesan cheese,
to serve*

serves 4

This is just one of those dishes that, once tasted, never forgotten. Pappa al pomodoro is a Tuscan 'soup', although traditionally it is so thick you can almost eat it with a fork! This version is slightly more soup-like.

Put the tomatoes in a saucepan, add the stock, sugar, 2 tablespoons of the oil and the leaves from the oregano and most of the basil leaves, reserving a few for serving. Add a little salt and pepper, then heat slowly to boiling point. Reduce the heat, cover and simmer gently for 30 minutes.

Toast the bread on a preheated medium-hot barbecue or a stove-top grill pan until barred with brown. Rub the bread all over with the garlic, then transfer to a plate. Sprinkle with the remaining oil and, using a fork, mash well into the bread, breaking it into small bits.

Add the bread to the soup and stir over low heat for about 5 minutes until the bread has been evenly incorporated and the soup has thickened.

Add more salt and pepper to taste and serve hot, topped with a little grated Parmesan and the reserved basil leaves. This dish is also delicious served cold.

Put the bagna cauda – the 'hot bath' – of warm anchovy butter in the centre of the table with a basket of fresh summer vegetables, so everyone can just help themselves.

summer vegetables with bagna cauda

200 g fresh, young, summer vegetables for each serving, such as baby carrots, baby fennel bulbs, radishes, cherry tomatoes, baby courgettes, washed and trimmed

bagna cauda

50 g unsalted butter

3–4 large garlic cloves, crushed

50 g anchovies in oil, drained and chopped

200 ml extra virgin olive oil

serves 4–6

Arrange the trimmed vegetables in a basket or on a large platter.

To make the bagna cauda, put the butter and garlic in a small saucepan and heat gently. Simmer very slowly for 4–5 minutes until the garlic has softened, but not browned. Add the anchovies, stir well, then pour in the oil. Cook gently for a further 10 minutes, stirring occasionally, until the sauce is soft and almost creamy.

Transfer the sauce to a dish and serve at once with the selection of vegetables.

All the colours of the Italian flag are here – red, white and green. This makes a great start to a rustic summer meal. Bocconcini (meaning 'little bites') are tiny balls of mozzarella, which are the perfect size for bruschetta. If you can't find them, use regular mozzarella instead and cut it into cubes.

cherry tomato, bocconcini and basil bruschetta

Put 3 tablespoons of the olive oil and the balsamic vinegar in a bowl and whisk. Stir in the halved bocconcini or mozzarella cubes, tomatoes and torn basil leaves, then season to taste with salt and pepper.

To make the bruschetta, grill, toast or pan-grill the bread on both sides until lightly charred or toasted. Rub the top side of each slice with the cut garlic, then drizzle with ½ tablespoon olive oil.

Cover each slice of bruschetta with rocket and spoon over the tomatoes and mozzarella. Drizzle with the remaining olive oil, top with extra fresh basil leaves, if using, and serve.

4½ tablespoons extra virgin olive oil

1 teaspoon balsamic vinegar

12 bocconcini cheeses, halved, or 375 g regular mozzarella cheese, cubed

20 ripe cherry tomatoes or pomodorini (baby plum tomatoes), halved

a handful of torn fresh basil leaves, plus extra to serve (optional)

4 thick slices of country bread, preferably sourdough

2 garlic cloves, halved

125 g rocket

sea salt and freshly ground black pepper

serves 4

Radicchio, the bitter red Italian chicory, is used as a salad leaf and also cooked as a vegetable. The round-headed Verona variety is available all year round, while trevise, the version with long leaves, is usually available only during autumn and winter. If you can't find them, use another bitter green, such as frisée or escarole, instead. Teamed with velvety blue Gorgonzola and walnuts, this is an utterly irresistible combination.

radicchio with gorgonzola and walnuts

125–150 g Gorgonzola cheese

1 head of radicchio

1 head of trevise or other bitter green

2 tablespoons extra virgin olive oil (optional)

75 g shelled walnuts or pecans

freshly ground black pepper

serves 4

Slice or break the cheese into 5 cm wedges or chunks.

Separate the radicchio and trevise into leaves.

Arrange the leaves on small serving plates and drizzle with olive oil, if using. Add the Gorgonzola and walnuts or pecans, then serve, sprinkled with freshly ground black pepper.

Asparagus in season is pure delight and, whether it is the fine wild variety or the large cultivated type, it is considered a particular treat in Europe. Add the delicate sweetness of Parma ham, dried to crispness, and you have an unusual combination. Use white asparagus if you can find it (French and Italian greengrocers often stock this during early summer), though green asparagus is more usual.

asparagus with prosciutto

8 thin slices prosciutto, such as Parma ham, about 150–200 g

500 g bunch of thick asparagus

2 tablespoons extra virgin olive oil or lemon oil

a shallow baking sheet

serves 4

Before turning on the oven, hang the slices of prosciutto over the grids of the top oven rack. Slide the rack into the oven, then turn it on to 150°C (300°F) Gas 2. Leave for 20 minutes until the ham is dry and crisp. Remove carefully and set aside.

Using a vegetable peeler, peel 7 cm of the tough skin off the end of each asparagus spear, then snap off and discard any tough ends. Arrange the asparagus on a shallow baking sheet and sprinkle with the oil. Cook under a preheated grill for 6–8 minutes, or until the asparagus is wrinkled and tender.

Serve the asparagus with some of the hot oil from the grill pan and 2 prosciutto 'crisps' for each person.

marinated anchovies

People tend to be intimidated by these little fish, but have no fear, they are easy to prepare and taste simply divine. Soon, you will be using these little gems with everything.

150 g fresh anchovies*

100 ml good-quality white vinegar

3 garlic cloves, sliced

1 tablespoon chopped fresh flat leaf parsley

100 ml olive oil

serves 4

To clean the anchovies, run your finger down the belly side and open up the fish. Pull the spine from the head and separate it from the flesh. Remove the head. Wash the fish and pat dry on kitchen paper.

Put the anchovies in a plastic container and pour in the vinegar. Let marinate in the refrigerator overnight. Rinse the anchovies and put in a serving dish with the garlic, parsley and oil, cover and chill overnight in the refrigerator.

Return to room temperature before serving with bread or as an accompaniment to another dish. You can return them to the refrigerator to eat another day – they only get better with time.

*note If fresh anchovies are unavailable, use any small fish: aim for 6–8 cm long

A mousseline is a mousse of fish, shellfish or poultry lightened with cream and egg whites. When made with salmon, it is the most beautiful, elegant, golden-pink. It is amazingly easy to prepare too, with a spectacular effect that makes a very luxurious starter or posh picnic dish.

smoked and fresh salmon terrine

250 g skinless salmon fillet, cut into chunks

1 teaspoon finely grated unwaxed orange zest

2 teaspoons freshly squeezed orange juice

4 tablespoons chopped fresh dill or chervil

400 g smoked salmon

2 egg whites, chilled

150 ml whipping cream, chilled

freshly ground white pepper

red salad leaves, to serve

900 ml terrine, lightly oiled and base-lined with greaseproof paper

a roasting tin

serves 6

Put the chunks of fresh salmon in a food processor with the orange zest, orange juice, dill or chervil and plenty of pepper. Blend until smooth. Remove the bowl from the food processor, cover and chill in the refrigerator.

Meanwhile, roughly chop half the smoked salmon. Put the bowl back on the processor. With the machine running, add the egg whites through the feed tube, then the cream. Blend until thick and smooth – do not overwork or it will curdle. Scrape into a bowl, then stir in the chopped smoked salmon. Carefully fill the prepared terrine with the mixture, packing down well. Level the surface and cover the top with buttered greaseproof paper. Stand the terrine in a roasting tin and pour in hot water to come halfway up the sides. Bake in a preheated oven at 180°C (350°F) Gas 4 for 35–40 minutes until firm. Remove from the oven, let cool completely, then chill in the refrigerator.

Loosen the edges of the terrine with a thin knife and turn out onto a wooden board. Trim and tidy up the edges and pat dry. Wrap the terrine with the remaining smoked salmon, pressing down well, then transfer to a flat serving platter. Slice the terrine with a very sharp knife and serve with red salad leaves.

This classic tapas dish is served just about everywhere in Spain. To make sure the end result is tender, buy small squid and don't cook them for too long.

fried squid roman-style

500 g small squid, or
150 g cleaned
squid tubes

2 eggs

plain flour, for dusting

olive oil, for frying

sea salt

1 lemon, cut into
wedges, to serve

an electric deep-fryer

serves 4

To clean the squid, pull the head away from the body (tube). Rub your thumb down the length of the tube and lever off the wings and discard. Remove the translucent quill inside and rub the pinky skin off the outside. Wash well under cold water. Cut the tubes into 1 cm slices.

Put the eggs in a bowl, add 2 tablespoons water and beat well. Put the flour on a plate and sprinkle generously with salt. Working on one squid ring at a time, dip them into the egg mixture, then into the flour, making sure they are well coated. Set aside.

Fill a deep-fryer with oil to the manufacturer's recommended level and heat to 195°C (380°F). Working in batches, cook the squid rings until golden brown. (Make sure the temperature remains the same for each batch.) Remove with a slotted spoon and drain on crumpled kitchen paper. Let rest for 5 minutes, then serve with the lemon wedges.

Yoghurt-crusted chicken threaded onto skewers makes ideal finger food for an informal start to a meal. The yoghurt tenderizes the chicken and helps the lemon soak into the meat. For the best flavour, cook them on a barbecue – the yoghurt becomes slightly crunchy. Delicious.

chicken lemon skewers

Cut the chicken fillets lengthways into 2 mm strips and put them in a shallow ceramic dish.

Put all the marinade ingredients in a bowl and stir well. Pour the marinade over the chicken, turn to coat, cover and let marinate in the refrigerator overnight.

The next day, thread the chicken onto the soaked bamboo skewers, zig-zagging the meat back and forth as you go.

Cook on a preheated barbecue or under a hot grill for 3–4 minutes on each side until charred and tender. Let cool slightly before serving.

500 g skinless chicken breast fillets

marinade

250 ml plain yoghurt

2 tablespoons extra virgin olive oil

2 garlic cloves, crushed

grated zest and freshly squeezed juice of 1 unwaxed lemon

1–2 teaspoons chilli powder

1 tablespoon chopped fresh coriander

sea salt and freshly ground black pepper

12 bamboo skewers, soaked in cold water for 30 minutes

serves 4

This tapas dish is simple and delicious. Chorizo comes in many different varieties – smoked, unsmoked, fresh and cured. Here, try using spicy chorizo, the size of regular breakfast sausages. Large quantities of paprika give a rich colour and pungent flavour.

chorizo in red wine

1 tablespoon olive oil

300 g small, spicy fresh chorizo sausages, cut into 1 cm slices

100 ml red wine

crusty bread, to serve

serves 4

Put the oil in a heavy-based frying pan and heat until smoking. Add the chorizo and cook for 1 minute. Reduce the heat, add the wine and cook for a further 5 minutes.

Transfer to a serving dish and set aside for a few minutes to develop the flavours. Serve warm with crusty bread.

salads

The famous Italian caprese salad normally includes basil. In this variation, rocket adds an intriguing, peppery bite. Do use milky, soft *mozzarella di bufala*, made from the rich, very white milk of water buffaloes, not cows. Add red-ripe, flavourful tomatoes and a good-quality extra virgin olive oil and this dish becomes sublime.

mozzarella, tomato and rocket salad

Drain the mozzarellas. Slice thickly or pull them apart into big rough chunks, showing the grainy strands. Arrange down one side of a large serving platter.

Slice the tomatoes thickly and arrange them in a second line down the middle of the plate. If they are very large, cut them in half first, then into semi-circles. Add the wild rocket leaves down the other side of the platter.

Sprinkle with salt and pepper, then just before serving trickle the olive oil over the top. Make sure you have crusty bread (slightly char-grilled tastes good) to mop up the juices.

variation Sharp, herby black olives may also be added.

3 buffalo mozzarella cheeses, 150 g each

4 large, juicy, sun-ripened red tomatoes

4 large handfuls of wild rocket, about 350 g

6–8 tablespoons extra virgin olive oil, preferably Italian

sea salt and freshly ground black pepper

crusty bread, to serve

serves 4

caesar salad

This is probably the most famous salad in the world and the perfect combination of salty, crispy crunch. It seems to have been around forever, but not so – it was invented by Italian chef Caesar Cardini in Tijuana, Mexico, in 1924. Note that this recipe serves one person – just multiply the ingredients to serve more people.

1 egg, preferably free range and organic

6 smallest leaves of cos lettuce (a young cos, not Little Gem)

½ tablespoon freshly squeezed lemon juice

2 tablespoons extra virgin olive oil

3–4 canned anchovy fillets, rinsed and drained

Parmesan cheese, at room temperature, shaved into curls with a vegetable peeler

sea salt and freshly ground black pepper

1 lemon cut into wedges, to serve (optional)

croutons

1 thick slice crusty white bread or challah bread

1 garlic clove, crushed

2 tablespoons oil or softened butter

serves 1

To cook the egg, put it in a small saucepan of water and bring to the boil. Reduce the heat and simmer for 4–5 minutes. Remove from the heat and cover with cold water to stop further cooking. Let cool a little, then peel. Cut into quarters just before serving.

To make the croutons. tear the bread into bite-sized chunks,* rub with the garlic and brush with oil or butter. Cook on a preheated stove-top grill pan until crisply golden and barred with brown.

Put the lettuce in a large bowl and sprinkle with salt and pepper, add the lemon juice and toss with your hands. Sprinkle with olive oil and toss again.

Put the croutons in a serving bowl and put the dressed leaves on top. Add the anchovies, egg quarters and Parmesan, sprinkle with pepper and serve with lemon wedges, if using.

*note The croutons were traditionally made of sliced bread cut into cubes. Here they are made freeform, so you get lots of crisp, crunchy edges. Be classic if you prefer.

Avocado is so creamy and delicious it can really be used as a dressing in itself. You can mix avocado with whatever looks good that day – crab, prawns, smoked fish, smoked chicken – top it just with a few herb leaves, lots of pepper, a squeeze of lemon juice and eat it without any dressing. If you have to share it with others, by all means serve it with these salad leaves and a regular dressing.

avocado salad

6 very thin slices smoked pancetta or bacon, or about 200 g pancetti cubes (lardons)

1 tablespoon olive oil

250 g salad leaves, a mixture of soft, crisp and peppery

1–2 ripe Hass avocados,* halved and stones removed

dressing

6 tablespoons extra virgin olive oil

1 tablespoon cider vinegar or rice vinegar

1 garlic clove, crushed

1 teaspoon Dijon mustard

sea salt and freshly ground black pepper

serves 4

If using pancetta, cut the slices into 3–4 pieces. Heat a frying pan, brush with 1 tablespoon olive oil, add the pancetta or pancetti and cook over medium heat, without disturbing the pancetta, until crisp on one side. Using tongs, turn the slices over and fry until crisp and papery but not too brown. Remove from the pan and drain on kitchen paper.

To make the dressing, put the oil, vinegar, garlic, mustard and salt and pepper in a salad bowl and beat with a fork or small whisk. When ready to serve, add the leaves and toss well, using your hands. Using a teaspoon, scoop out balls of avocado into the salad. Toss gently if you like (though this will send the avocado to the bottom of the bowl). Add the crispy pancetta or pancetti and serve immediately.

*note To test an avocado for ripeness, don't stick your thumb in it. Cradle it in the palm of your hand and squeeze gently. If it just gives to the pressure, it's perfect.

Greek salads are so much part of the easy, Mediterranean style of eating – a bit of crisp, a bit of fiery, a few baby herbs, some vinegary olives (and Greece produces some of the best) and salty anchovies. Unpitted Kalamata olives are used in the recipe because they have more flavour. However, you had better warn your guests in case they're not expecting them.

big greek salad

1 iceberg lettuce, quartered and torn apart

about 250 g feta cheese, crumbled into big pieces, or cut into cubes

about 200 g Kalamata olives

2 red onions, halved, then sliced

2 mini cucumbers, halved lengthways, then thinly sliced diagonally

4 big ripe red tomatoes, cut into chunks

8 fresh anchovy fillets*, or to taste

a few sprigs of oregano, torn

a few sprigs of mint, torn

greek dressing

6 tablespoons extra virgin olive oil, preferably Greek

2 tablespoons freshly squeezed lemon juice

sea salt and freshly ground black pepper

serves 4

Put the lettuce in a big bowl. Add the feta, olives, onions, cucumbers and tomatoes.

To make the dressing, put the olive oil, lemon juice, salt and pepper in a jug or bowl and beat with a fork, then pour it over the salad.

Top with the anchovies, oregano and mint, and serve.

*note If you don't have a Greek deli and can't get hold of fresh anchovies, use canned ones instead. Rinse and drain them before adding them to the salad.

A beautiful, delicious, simple salad based on the classic *Insalata Caprese*. If you can't find the most important ingredient for the original salad (the very best, ripest, most flavourful tomatoes), peppers are a great solution.

italian grilled pepper salad

4 large red peppers, preferably the long, pointed kind (romano or ramira)

4 tablespoons best-quality, extra virgin olive oil

2 mozzarella cheeses, preferably buffalo mozzarella, 150 g each

4 handfuls of wild rocket

balsamic vinegar (optional)

sea salt and freshly ground black pepper

serves 4

Put the whole peppers under a hot grill, on a barbecue or over the flame of a gas stove. Cook on all sides until charred. Remove from the heat, transfer to a saucepan and put on the lid (this will help steam off the skins).

When cool, drain the juices into a small bowl. Scrape off and discard the charred skins. Cut the peppers in half lengthways and scrape out and discard the seeds and membranes, adding any juices to the bowl.

To make the dressing, put 2 tablespoons of the pepper juices in another bowl with the olive oil and beat with a fork. Add salt and pepper to taste and extra pepper juice if you like. (Keep any extra juice for another use.)

When ready to assemble the salad, tear the mozzarellas into big shreds – about 4 pieces each – and divide among 4 chilled plates. Add a handful of rocket and 2 pepper halves to each plate. Sprinkle with the dressing, then add a few drops of balsamic,* if using, to each serving. Sprinkle with sea salt flakes and pepper and serve.

*note Don't slather the balsamic over the salad. Use it as a seasoning, not a dressing.

6 very ripe plum tomatoes

2 garlic cloves, thinly sliced

4 thick slices day-old bread, preferably Italian-style, such as ciabatta

about 10 cm cucumber, halved, deseeded and thinly sliced diagonally

1 red onion, chopped

1 tablespoon chopped fresh flat leaf parsley

8–12 tablespoons extra virgin olive oil

2 tablespoons white wine vinegar, cider vinegar or sherry vinegar

a bunch of basil, leaves torn

12 caperberries or 4 tablespoons capers packed in brine, rinsed and drained

1 teaspoon balsamic vinegar (optional)

sea salt and freshly ground black pepper

serves 4

There are as many variations of this Tuscan bread salad as there are cooks. The trick is to let the flavours blend well without allowing the bread to disintegrate into a mush. Always use the ripest, reddest, most flavourful tomatoes you can find, such as sweet Marmande, one of the full-flavoured heirloom varieties – Black Russian or Green Zebra – or at least an Italian plum tomato.

tuscan panzanella

Cut the tomatoes in half, spike with slivers of garlic and roast in a preheated oven at 180°C (350°F) Gas 4 for about 1 hour or until wilted and some of the moisture has evaporated.

Meanwhile, put the bread on an oiled stove-top grill pan and cook on both sides until lightly toasted and barred with grill marks. Tear or cut the toast into pieces and put in a salad bowl. Sprinkle with a little water until damp.

Add the tomatoes, cucumber, onion, parsley, salt and pepper. Sprinkle with the olive oil and vinegar, toss well, then set aside for about 1 hour to develop the flavours.

Add the basil leaves, caperberries or capers and balsamic vinegar, if using, then serve.

quick chickpea salad

1 kg cooked or canned
chickpeas, rinsed and drained

4 marinated artichoke hearts

4 large sun-blushed (semi-dried)
tomatoes (optional)*

250 g very ripe cherry
tomatoes, halved

8 spring onions, sliced diagonally

a handful of fresh basil
leaves, torn

a small bunch of fresh chives,
scissor-snipped

leaves from 4 sprigs of flat leaf
parsley, chopped

50 g Parmesan cheese, shaved

1 tablespoon black peppercorns,
cracked with a mortar and pestle

dijon dressing

6 tablespoons extra virgin
olive oil

1 tablespoon freshly squeezed
lemon juice or sherry vinegar

1 teaspoon Dijon mustard

1 small garlic clove, crushed

sea salt and freshly ground
black pepper

serves 4

Chickpeas are a great ingredient for lunchtime salads and as an accompaniment to main courses. Like all dried pulses, they drink up flavours, but unlike some, chickpeas can be relied upon not to fall apart. They're perfect for picnics and other make-ahead occasions. You can part-prepare them, so the dressing soaks into the chickpeas, then add the fresh ingredients just before serving.

To make the dressing, put the oil, lemon juice or vinegar, mustard, garlic and salt and pepper in a bowl and beat with a fork. Add the chickpeas, artichoke hearts and sun-blushed tomatoes, if using, and toss in the dressing. Cover and chill in the refrigerator for up to 4 hours.

When ready to serve, add the cherry tomatoes, spring onions, basil, chives and parsley. Stir gently, sprinkle with the shaved Parmesan and cracked peppercorns, then serve.

*note Sun-blushed tomatoes, which are partly sun-dried tomatoes, are sold in Italian delis.

variations You can add any number of other ingredients, including olives, Parma ham, salami or chorizo, canned or char-grilled fresh tuna, other vegetables, leaves or herbs, or your favourite spices.

A few drops of chilli oil in the dressing instead of the mustard give a different kind of fire.

Tabbouleh, the fresh parsley salad from Lebanon, is based on bulghur wheat. This version is made with couscous, the fine Moroccan pasta, now available in an instant version – you just soak it in water or stock for about 10 minutes.

fragrant herb couscous salad

300 g instant couscous

freshly squeezed juice
of 1 lemon

2 tablespoons chopped fresh
basil leaves

2 tablespoons chopped
fresh coriander

2 tablespoons chopped fresh
mint leaves

2 tablespoons chopped
fresh parsley

sea salt and freshly ground
black pepper

2 lemons, halved, to serve
(optional)

fragrant garlic oil

1 whole head of garlic,
cloves separated

2 bay leaves

600 ml extra virgin olive oil

serves 4

To make the fragrant oil, peel the garlic cloves and put them in a saucepan. Add the bay leaves and oil and heat gently for 15 minutes until the garlic has softened. Don't let the garlic brown. Let cool, remove and mash the garlic cloves, then return them to the oil. Refrigerate until required. Use 150 ml garlic oil for this recipe and reserve the remainder.

Put the couscous in a bowl, add water to cover by 5 cm and let soak for 10 minutes.

Drain the soaked couscous, shaking the sieve well to remove any excess water. Transfer to a bowl, add the 150 ml fragrant garlic oil, lemon juice, chopped basil, coriander, mint and parsley. Season with salt and pepper, then set aside to develop the flavours until ready to serve. Serve with halved lemons, if using.

New Zealanders go wild about these white, marble-sized new potatoes. They are mostly consumed locally, but a small surplus is exported to Australia and California. When you have grown bored with eating them plain, or with butter or olive oil and herbs, there are some other interesting dressings to explore. This one includes canned smoked oysters, fresh lime juice and superb extra virgin olive oil – though it looks messy and odd, it tastes gorgeous.

antipodean potato salad

750 g marble-sized new potatoes, scrubbed

160 ml extra virgin olive oil

85 g canned smoked oysters, drained

2 teaspoons Dijon mustard

freshly squeezed juice of 1 lime

2 garlic cloves, crushed

2–3 teaspoons mild paprika

sea salt flakes and freshly ground black pepper

a bunch of fresh chives, scissor-snipped, or a few sprigs of basil, to serve

serves 6

Cook the potatoes in boiling salted water for 15–18 minutes or until tender. Drain. Crush them very gently and lightly with a fork, then return them to the still-hot pan. Drizzle with about half the olive oil, then sprinkle with salt and pepper.

To make the dressing, put the remaining oil, smoked oysters, mustard, lime juice, garlic and paprika in a blender and process to form a creamy emulsion. Trickle half the dressing over the warm potatoes and serve the rest separately. Sprinkle the potatoes with chives or basil, then serve warm or cool.

variation For a sensational shocking pink salad dressing, omit the smoked oysters and use another famous New Zealand product, the tamarillo, instead. Cut 2 ripe tamarillos in half and scoop out the red flesh. Blend with the other dressing ingredients for a vivid, colourful vegetarian dressing.

salade niçoise

10–12 small salad potatoes, such as Pink Fir Apples or Charlottes

olive oil, for tossing the potatoes

4 small eggs

100 g shelled broad beans, fresh or frozen, or 6 cooked baby artichokes, halved

100 g green beans, trimmed

3 spring onions, halved lengthways

2 small red onions, halved lengthways

2 mini cucumbers or 20 cm regular cucumber, unwaxed

2 red or yellow peppers, peeled (see method)

4 Little Gem baby lettuces or other soft lettuce leaves

1 punnet cherry tomatoes, about 20, halved

1 small can anchovy fillets, drained or 1 large can or jar good-quality tuna, drained

about 20 black olives, preferably Niçoise

about 20 caperberries or 3 tablespoons salt-packed capers, rinsed and drained

a large handful of fresh basil leaves

vinaigrette

6 tablespoons extra virgin olive oil

1 tablespoon white wine vinegar, cider vinegar or sherry vinegar

1 teaspoon Dijon mustard (optional)

1 garlic clove, crushed

sea salt and freshly ground black pepper

serves 8 as a starter, 4 as a main course

A classic composed salad from the south of France, this salade Niçoise makes a wonderful lunch for four or a starter for eight.

Cook the potatoes in boiling salted water until tender, about 10 minutes. Drain and plunge them into a bowl of iced water with ice cubes. Let cool. Drain, then toss in a little olive oil and cut in half.

Put the eggs in a saucepan of cold water, bring to the boil, reduce the heat and simmer for 5 minutes. Drain, then cover with cold water. When cool, peel, then cut in half just before serving.

Steam the broad beans, if using, and green beans separately until tender. Plunge into iced water, then pop each broad bean out of its grey skin. Blanch the spring onions for 30 seconds in boiling water. Drain and plunge into the iced water. Alternatively, leave uncooked.

Thinly slice the red onions and cucumbers, preferably on a mandoline – slice the cucumbers diagonally. If peeling the peppers, do so using a vegetable peeler, then cut off the top and bottom, open out, deseed and cut the flesh into thick strips.

Put the lettuce leaves on a platter. Add bundles of green beans and spring onions, then the potatoes, broad beans or artichokes, halved eggs, tomatoes, cucumber, onions and peppers. Top with anchovy fillets or tuna, black olives, caperberries or capers and basil leaves.

To make the vinaigrette, mix all the ingredients in a small jug and serve separately.

Tonno e fagioli – tuna and beans. This is a simple Italian dish that's great when you come home from work, all the shops have shut, and you've run out of almost everything. Though any dolphin-friendly canned tuna is fine, it will be fabulously good if you use top-quality French or Italian tuna, usually sold in jars, not cans. Cannellini beans can be delicate, so toss them gently. Though not traditional, you could make this with chickpeas, lentils, borlotti beans or green flageolets instead of the cannellini beans.

tonno e fagioli

1–2 fat garlic cloves

1 tablespoon sherry vinegar or white wine vinegar

6 tablespoons extra virgin olive oil

600 g cooked or canned cannellini beans, rinsed and drained

2 red onions, thinly sliced into petals, then blanched*, or 6 small spring onions, sliced

400 g best-quality tuna

a few handfuls of fresh basil leaves

sea salt and freshly ground black pepper

serves 6

Put the garlic on a chopping board, crush with the flat of a knife, add a large pinch of salt, then mash to a paste with the tip of the knife. Transfer to a bowl, add the vinegar and 2 tablespoons of the oil and beat with a fork.

Add the beans and onions and toss gently. Taste, then add extra oil and vinegar to taste.

Drain the tuna and separate into large chunks. Add to the bowl and turn gently to coat with the dressing. Top with the basil leaves and black pepper to serve.

*note Blanching is optional, but it takes the edge off the sharpness of the onions. To blanch them, put them in a saucepan of boiling water, boil for 1 minute, then remove from the heat and drain well.

With its rich, almost plum-like flavours of raisins and Marsala, this salad is a real treat. Sherry vinegar is sold in larger supermarkets or delicatessens. If you can't find it, use balsamic instead.

chicken salad
with radicchio and pine nuts

Put the onion slices in a small bowl and cover with cold water. Let soak for 30 minutes, drain well, then dry thoroughly with kitchen paper.

Tear or slice the chicken into thin strips and put in a large salad bowl. Add the radicchio, rocket, parsley and onion.

To make the dressing, put 2 tablespoons of the oil in a frying pan and heat gently. Add the raisins and pine nuts and sauté for 3–4 minutes until the pine nuts are lightly golden. Add the Marsala and vinegar, with salt and pepper to taste, and warm through. Stir in the remaining oil and remove from the heat.

Pour the dressing over the salad, toss lightly and serve.

1 small red onion, sliced
750 g cooked chicken breast
1 head of radicchio, shredded
125 g rocket
a few sprigs of flat leaf parsley

marsala raisin dressing
100 ml extra virgin olive oil
75 g raisins
50 g pine nuts
2 tablespoons Marsala wine
2 tablespoons sherry vinegar
sea salt and freshly ground black pepper

serves 4–6

One great thing about many Thai dishes is their use of fresh herbs. They are often flooded with the pungent flavours of Thai basil, mint and coriander. Thai basil is available from Asian stores, but you could use ordinary basil instead. Bok choy is also known as 'pak choi'.

thai-style beef salad

1 tablespoon Szechuan peppercorns, or black peppercorns, lightly crushed

1 teaspoon ground coriander

1 teaspoon sea salt

500 g beef fillet, in one piece

1 tablespoon peanut oil or vegetable oil

1 cucumber, thinly sliced

4 spring onions, thinly sliced

2 baby bok choy, thinly sliced

a handful of fresh Thai basil leaves

a handful of fresh mint leaves

a handful of fresh coriander

lime dressing

15 g palm sugar or brown sugar

1 tablespoon fish sauce

2 tablespoons freshly squeezed lime juice

2 red chillies, deseeded and chopped

1 garlic clove, crushed

serves 4

Put the peppercorns, ground coriander and salt onto a plate and mix. Rub the beef all over with the oil, then put onto the plate and turn to coat with the spices.

Cook the beef on a preheated barbecue or stove-top grill pan for about 10 minutes, turning to brown evenly. Remove from the heat and let cool.

Meanwhile, to make the dressing, put the sugar in a saucepan, add the fish sauce and 2 tablespoons water and heat until the sugar dissolves. Remove the pan from the heat, let cool, then stir in the lime juice, chillies and garlic.

Cut the beef into thin slices and transfer to a large bowl. Add the cucumber, spring onions, bok choy and herbs. Pour over the dressing, toss well and serve.

picnics

Black olives, which have already been cured, will mellow even more if you crack them a little or prick with a fork, then marinate in aromatics and fine olive oil as they do in Morocco. Experiment until you find a flavour you like – your own customized blend. If you were to use Moroccan oil in this recipe, the result would be really authentic, but any robust extra virgin will do.

marinated black olives

750 g black olives in brine

2 tablespoons fennel or cumin seeds, crushed

1 tablespoon green cardamom pods, crushed

1 tablespoon small hot dried red chillies

2 tablespoons allspice berries, crushed

850 ml extra virgin olive oil

20 cm strip of orange zest, bruised

12 fresh bay leaves, washed, dried and bruised

1 large jar, 1.5 litres, or 3 jars, 500 ml each, sterilized (page 4)

makes 1.5 litres

Rinse the olives in cold water, drain, then pat dry with kitchen paper.

Put them on a clean dry surface such as a chopping board and crush them slightly with a meat hammer or rolling pin, or prick with a fork, to open up the flesh a little.

Put the fennel or cumin, cardamom, chillies and allspice in a dry frying pan and toast over moderate heat for a few minutes until aromatic.

Put the olive oil in a saucepan and heat to 180°C (350°F) – a cube of bread should turn golden-brown in 40–50 seconds. Let cool a little. Using a sterilized spoon, pack the zest, bay leaves, olives and spices into the jar, or jars, in layers, until they all have been used. Cover with the hot olive oil. Let cool, uncovered. When cold, seal the jars and store in a cool, dark place.

Leave for at least 1 week before tasting. They will keep well and improve for some months.

With its lovely, earthy flavours, a frittata is an Italian version of the Spanish tortilla or the French omelette and different ingredients are added depending on the region or season.

mixed mushroom frittata

3 tablespoons extra virgin olive oil

2 shallots, finely chopped

2 garlic cloves, finely chopped

1 tablespoon chopped fresh thyme leaves

300 g mixed wild and cultivated mushrooms, such as girolle, chanterelle, portobello, shiitake and cep

6 eggs

2 tablespoons chopped fresh flat leaf parsley

sea salt and freshly ground black pepper

serves 6

Put 2 tablespoons of the oil in a non-stick frying pan, heat gently, then add the shallots, garlic and thyme. Fry gently for 5 minutes until softened but not browned.

Meanwhile, brush off any dirt clinging to the mushrooms and wipe the caps. Chop or slice coarsely and add to the pan. Fry for 4–5 minutes until they are just starting to release their juices. Remove from the heat.

Put the eggs in a bowl with the parsley and a little salt and pepper, whisk briefly, then stir in the mushroom mixture. Wipe the frying pan clean.

Heat the remaining 1 tablespoon of oil in the clean pan and pour in the egg and mushroom mixture. Cook over medium heat for 8–10 minutes until set on the bottom. Transfer the pan to a preheated grill and cook for 2–3 minutes until the top of the frittata is set and spotted brown. Remove from the heat and let cool. Wrap in parchment paper for transporting.

Other breads can be used in these fantastic, fresh-tasting pizzas, so don't go shopping specially for ciabatta. You can also use Cheddar or blue cheese instead of mozzarella.

toasted ciabatta pizzas

Toast the ciabatta under a hot grill until lightly golden, then rub with the garlic, using it like a grater. Put the garlic ciabatta on a baking sheet and drizzle with a little of the olive oil.

Arrange the sliced tomatoes on the bread, then add the olives, marjoram, mozzarella, basil, salt and pepper. Drizzle more oil over the top.

Cook in a preheated oven at 180°C (350°F) Gas 4 for 15–20 minutes until the tomatoes are softened and crisp around the edges and the mozzarella has melted. Remove from the oven, let cool and wrap in parchment paper before packing.

1 loaf ciabatta, split lengthways or sliced

1 garlic clove, peeled

about 4 tablespoons olive oil

4 ripe tomatoes, skinned and sliced

a handful of pitted olives

a bunch of marjoram

2 balls mozzarella cheese

a bunch of basil

sea salt and freshly ground black pepper

a baking sheet

serves 4

This quick and simple salad sparkles with the good, clean, peppery taste of watercress and the delicious crunch of radish and celery.

summer salad

300 g watercress, ends trimmed

a bunch of radishes, trimmed and halved

6 celery stalks, sliced

4 tablespoons olive oil

2 tablespoons balsamic vinegar

sea salt and freshly ground black pepper

serves 4

Put the watercress in a large plastic container, then add the halved radishes and sliced celery.

Put the olive oil, vinegar and salt and pepper to taste in a screw-top jar. Just before serving, shake the dressing well, drizzle over the salad, toss well and serve immediately.

note Some salad items are not good travellers and by the time they make it from your shopping basket to your kitchen, they may have seen better days. Replace any of the ingredients in the above salad with whatever is fresh and best in the market on the day: remember shopping should always be flexible.

Orzo is a rice-shaped pasta, ideal for making
into a salad because it retains its shape and
texture really well when cooked.

orzo salad
with lemon and herb dressing

250 g cherry tomatoes, halved

6 tablespoons extra virgin olive oil

250 g orzo or other tiny soup pasta*

6 spring onions, finely chopped

4 tablespoons coarsely chopped mixed fresh herbs, such as basil, dill, mint and parsley

grated zest and juice of 2 unwaxed lemons

sea salt and freshly ground black pepper

4 wooden skewers, soaked in cold water for 30 minutes

serves 4

Thread the tomatoes onto the soaked wooden skewers with all the cut halves facing the same way. Sprinkle with a little olive oil, season with salt and pepper and cook under a preheated hot grill for 1–2 minutes on each side until lightly charred and softened.

Bring a large saucepan of water to the boil. Add a large pinch of salt, then the orzo and cook for about 9 minutes or until *al dente*. Drain well and transfer to a large bowl.

Heat 2 tablespoons of the olive oil in a frying pan, add the spring onions, herbs and lemon zest and stir-fry for 30 seconds. Add the mixture to the orzo, then add the tomatoes, lemon juice, remaining olive oil, salt and pepper. Toss well and let cool before serving.

*note Orzo is available from many large supermarkets and Italian delicatessens. If unavailable, use other pasta shapes instead.

chicken and tarragon pesto pasta

300 g dried penne pasta

4 tablespoons olive oil

3 cooked chicken breasts, sliced

100 g rocket

sea salt and freshly ground black pepper

tarragon pesto

75 g Parmesan cheese, freshly grated

75 g pan-toasted pine nuts

a large bunch of tarragon, leaves stripped from the stem and chopped

grated zest and juice of 1 unwaxed lemon

1 garlic clove, crushed and chopped

5 tablespoons olive oil

serves 4

This really is a great dish – tarragon and chicken go together so well. Kids will love it, yet it tastes good enough for adults to tuck into as well. Pesto can be made out of most herbs, so don't hesitate to try your favourites in this recipe and blend to create your own version.

Bring a large saucepan of water to the boil. Add a large pinch of salt, then the pasta, stir and cook for about 10 minutes or until *al dente*. Drain and refresh the pasta in cold water, then drain thoroughly and toss in the oil.

To make the tarragon pesto, put the Parmesan, pine nuts, tarragon, lemon zest and juice, garlic and oil in a jug and purée until smooth with a hand-held blender.

Put the pasta, pesto, chicken and rocket in a serving bowl, season with salt and pepper and toss well, coating the pasta and chicken evenly with the pesto. Serve immediately.

notes When taking this salad on a picnic, don't add the rocket until just before eating or the oil will make it wilt.

If you don't want meat, replace the chicken with steamed vegetables such as courgettes, sugarsnap peas, broad beans or runner beans.

This salad has travelled all over the world and many additions to the basic lettuce and croutons with cheese and anchovy dressing can be found. Transforming the salad into a wrap makes a great idea for a picnic dish.

chicken caesar wrap

3 large slices of smoked bacon

250 g cooked chicken breast

6 small flour tortillas

300 g cos lettuce, shredded (inner leaves only)

12 anchovy fillets in oil, drained and chopped

caesar dressing

1 egg yolk

1 tablespoon freshly squeezed lemon juice

1 teaspoon Worcestershire sauce

150 ml olive oil

25 g freshly grated Parmesan cheese

sea salt and freshly ground black pepper

serves 6

Grill or fry the bacon for 2–3 minutes until crisp. Let cool, then cut into thin strips. Roughly shred the chicken into large strips.

To make the dressing, put the egg yolk in a small bowl, add the lemon juice, Worcestershire sauce and a little salt and pepper and whisk until frothy. Gradually whisk in the oil, a little at a time, until thickened and glossy. Add 2 tablespoons water to thin the sauce, then stir in the cheese.

Lay one tortilla flat on a work surface and arrange a little lettuce down the middle of it. Top with chicken, bacon, anchovies, a spoonful of the dressing and, finally, more lettuce. Wrap the tortilla into a roll, then wrap the roll in a napkin. Repeat to make 6 wraps. Chill in the refrigerator to serve later.

tiger prawns
with herb mayonnaise

*1 kg cooked
tiger prawns*

*lemon wedges, to serve
(optional)*

herb mayonnaise

2 egg yolks

*1 tablespoon freshly
squeezed lemon juice*

*1 teaspoon Dijon
mustard*

300 ml olive oil

*4 tablespoons chopped
fresh mixed herbs, such
as basil, chives, chervil,
dill, parsley and tarragon*

*sea salt and freshly
ground black pepper*

serves 6

Summer and picnics are all about this type of simple, delicious, messy food. Peel big, juicy, cooked prawns, then dunk them in a bowl of wonderful home-made herb mayonnaise. Use a plain olive oil, rather than extra virgin for mayonnaise, or it can be rather bitter.

To make the herb mayonnaise, put the egg yolks, lemon juice, mustard and a little salt and pepper in a food processor and blend briefly until frothy. With the motor running, slowly pour the oil through the feed tube to make a thick, glossy sauce. If it becomes too thick, add a little warm water to thin it. Add the chopped herbs and blend again until the mayonnaise is a vibrant speckled green.

Peel the prawns and serve with the mayonnaise and wedges of lemon, if using.

vegetables & vegetarian dishes

grilled corn
with chilli salt rub

6 ears of corn, husks removed and ends trimmed

2 tablespoons extra virgin olive oil, plus extra to serve

3 ancho chillies

1½ tablespoons sea salt

3 limes, cut into wedges

serves 6

One of the America's most popular chillies is the ancho, the dried version of the poblano. When ground to a fine powder, it has a smoky flavour and is mild to medium on the heat scale – delicious with the sweet, nutty taste of corn.

Bring a large saucepan of lightly salted water to the boil, add the corn and boil for 5 minutes. Drain and refresh under cold water. Pat dry.

Preheat a barbecue or grill until hot. Brush the corn with oil and cook on the barbecue or under the grill for 6–8 minutes, turning frequently until charred all over.

Meanwhile, remove the stalk and seeds from the dried chillies. Chop the flesh coarsely and, using a spice grinder or mortar and pestle, grind to a powder. Transfer to a small bowl, then mix in the salt.

Rub the lime wedges vigorously over the corn, sprinkle with the chilli salt and serve with extra oil for drizzling.

If you can find them, use the little Asian aubergines to make this dish – they look very pretty and have a more interesting texture than large aubergines. When buying herbs, try going to independent greengrocers or market stalls where they are sold in big bunches – these herbs taste better and are much better value.

baked aubergines
with pesto sauce

300 g small aubergines
4 tablespoons olive oil
basil pesto (page 228)

a baking sheet, lightly oiled

serves 4

Cut the aubergines in half lengthways and put on the baking sheet. Drizzle with a little oil and bake in a preheated oven at 190°C (375°F) Gas 5 for 15–20 minutes, then turn them over and cook for a further 15 minutes.

When the aubergines are cooked, transfer them to a serving dish, drizzle with the pesto and serve hot or cold.

note Make twice the quantity of pesto and store the extra in the refrigerator – it always comes in handy as an easy salad dressing or tossed through pasta for a quick, delicious supper. Keep the pesto covered with a thin film of olive oil and it will stay fresh for several weeks.

Use purple basil if you can find it because it looks even more spectacular than green. This dish really couldn't be easier, and makes an interesting alternative to plain roast tomatoes.

mozzarella baked tomatoes

20 ripe tomatoes

250 g mozzarella cheese, drained and cut into 20 pieces

100 ml olive oil

a bunch of basil, leaves torn

sea salt and freshly ground black pepper

a large baking sheet, lightly oiled

serves 20

Cut a deep cross, to about halfway down, in the top of each tomato and push a piece of mozzarella into each one. Transfer to the baking sheet and sprinkle with salt and pepper.

Cook in a preheated oven at 160°C (325°F) Gas 3 for 25 minutes until the tomatoes are beginning to soften and open up.

Sprinkle with oil and basil leaves and serve warm.

Basil oil is particularly good sprinkled onto this simple pastry,
but you can use ordinary olive oil. Preheating the baking sheet
will make the base of the tart beautifully crisp.

simple tomato and olive tart
with basil oil

*350 g ready-made puff
pastry, thawed if frozen*

*125 g red cherry tomatoes,
halved*

*125 g yellow cherry
tomatoes, halved*

*50 g semi-dried or sun-dried
tomatoes, halved*

*50 g pitted black olives,
halved*

*25 g freshly grated
Parmesan cheese*

*sea salt and freshly ground
black pepper*

a handful of rocket, to serve

basil oil

25 g fresh basil leaves

150 ml extra virgin olive oil

2 baking sheets

serves 4

To make the basil oil, blanch the leaves very briefly in boiling water,
drain and pat dry with kitchen paper. Put in a blender, add the oil
and a pinch of salt and blend until very smooth. Strain through a
fine sieve, then refrigerate until needed. Return to room temperature
before using. You will need 2 tablespoons for this recipe.

Preheat the oven to 220°C (425°F) Gas 7 and put a baking sheet
on the middle shelf to heat up.

Roll out the pastry on a lightly floured work surface to form a
rectangle, 25 x 30 cm. Trim the edges and transfer the dough to
a second baking sheet. Using the blade of a sharp knife, gently
tap the edges horizontally several times (this will help the pastry
rise and the edges separate) and prick all over with a fork.

Put the tomatoes, olives, 2 tablespoons basil oil, salt and pepper
in a bowl and mix lightly. Spoon the mixture onto the pastry and
carefully slide the tart directly onto the preheated baking sheet.
Bake in the preheated oven for 12–15 minutes until risen and golden.

Remove from the oven and sprinkle with the Parmesan. Cut into
4 pieces and serve hot with a handful of rocket leaves.

Experiment with different fillings, for instance use sun-dried peppers instead of sun-dried tomatoes.

courgette quiche

Put all the pastry ingredients in a food processor and blend until the ingredients just come together. Tip the mixture onto a lightly floured work surface and bring the mixture together with your hands. Pat into a disc, wrap and chill it for 20 minutes.

Transfer the pastry to a lightly floured work surface and roll out to a disc just bigger than the tin. Line the tin with it and cut off excess pastry at the edges. Refrigerate for 15 minutes.

Line the pastry case with greaseproof paper and fill with baking beans or uncooked rice. Bake in a preheated oven at 200°C (400°F) Gas 6 for 10–15 minutes, then remove the greaseproof paper and beans and return the tart case to the oven for 3–5 minutes until just cooked. Remove from the oven and reduce the oven temperature to 180°C (350°F) Gas 4.

To make the filling, put a few drops of the oil in a frying pan and wipe it over the surface with kitchen paper. Heat until hot, add the courgettes and fry until golden on both sides.

Put the crème fraîche in a bowl, add the whole eggs and yolks and beat to mix. Add salt and pepper to taste. Arrange the courgette slices in the tart case, add the sun-dried tomatoes, then pour in the egg mixture. Bake in the preheated oven for 30–35 minutes until golden and set. Serve hot, warm or cold.

pastry

280 g plain flour, plus extra for dusting

a pinch of salt

140 g chilled butter, diced

2 egg yolks

2 tablespoons very cold water

filling

2 tablespoons olive oil

750 g courgettes, sliced diagonally

325 ml crème fraîche

2 whole eggs, plus 2 egg yolks

5–6 pieces sun-dried tomatoes in olive oil, drained and coarsely chopped

sea salt and freshly ground black pepper

a loose-based tart tin, 25 cm diameter

greaseproof paper and baking beans or uncooked rice

serves 8

fish, meat
& poultry

Meat and fish (the old-fashioned surf 'n' turf) can work well together, and this dish is an example of the perfect balance of strong flavours. This recipe uses the chorizo sausage that needs cooking, rather than the cured tapas variety, although either would do.

prawn, chorizo and sage skewers

300 g uncooked chorizo

24 large, uncooked, peeled prawns, deveined

24 large fresh sage leaves

extra virgin olive oil

freshly squeezed lemon juice

freshly ground black pepper

12 skewers, metal or bamboo (if using bamboo, soak them in warm water for 30 minutes)

serves 6

Cut the chorizo into 24 slices about 1 cm thick and thread onto the skewers, alternating with the prawns and sage leaves. Put a little oil and lemon juice in a small bowl, mix well, then drizzle over the skewers. Sprinkle with pepper.

Meanwhile, preheat an overhead grill, stove-top grill pan or barbecue until hot. Cook the skewers for 1½–2 minutes on each side until the chorizo and prawns are cooked through. Serve at once.

The squid will curl up as they cook, so use a pair of tongs to open them out again and press them flat. You could also put a heatproof plate on top to keep them that way. Take care not to overcook the squid or it will be tough.

seared squid with lemon and coriander dressing

4 medium squid, cleaned*, about 750 g

1 tablespoon extra virgin olive oil

sea salt and freshly ground black pepper

baby spinach leaves, to serve

lemon and coriander dressing

5 tablespoons peanut oil

1 tablespoon toasted sesame oil

freshly squeezed juice of 1 lemon

2 tablespoons sweet soy sauce (Indonesian kecap manis), or regular soy sauce with ½ teaspoon sugar

2 tablespoons chopped fresh coriander

1 garlic clove, crushed

serves 4

To make the dressing, put the oils, lemon juice, soy sauce, coriander and garlic in a screw-top jar, shake until well mixed and use as required. If storing in the refrigerator, omit the coriander and add it just before use.

Cut the squid bodies in half and open out flat. Brush with the olive oil and season with salt and pepper.

Heat a stove-top grill pan until very hot. Add the squid bodies and tentacles and cook for 1 minute on each side until charred and tender. Transfer to a wooden board and cut the squid into thick slices.

Put the dressing in a bowl, add the squid and toss well. Serve with a few baby spinach leaves and extra black pepper.

*note Squid is very easy to clean. To do so, pull out the tentacles (the insides should come with them). Cut off the tentacles and discard the insides. Rinse out the bodies, pulling out the stiff transparent quill, like a little wand of plastic.

salmon frittata
with potatoes and asparagus

A frittata is an Italian omelette cooked slowly over low heat, with the filling stirred into the eggs or spread over the top. It is served perfectly set, never folded, and makes a terrific lunchtime snack or party food.

250 g fresh asparagus, trimmed

175 g small new potatoes

6 free range organic eggs

50 g freshly grated Parmesan cheese

3 tablespoons chopped fresh mixed herbs

40 g butter

250 g fresh salmon, skinned and diced into large chunks

sea salt and freshly ground black pepper

a heavy-based, non-stick frying pan, 22 cm diameter

serves 2–4

Steam the asparagus for 12 minutes or until tender, plunge into cold water to set the colour and cool completely.

Cook the potatoes in a saucepan of boiling salted water for 15–20 minutes until tender. Drain, let cool, then slice thickly. Drain the asparagus, then dry it and cut into short lengths.

Put the eggs in a bowl with a pinch of salt, lots of pepper and half the Parmesan cheese and beat well. Stir in the asparagus and herbs. Melt the butter in the heavy-based, non-stick frying pan. When foaming, pour in the egg mixture then scatter the salmon all over. Turn down the heat as low as possible. Cook for about 15 minutes until the bottom is set, but with the top still a little runny.

Arrange the cooked sliced potato on top and sprinkle with the remaining Parmesan. Cook under a preheated hot grill until the cheese is lightly browned and the top is just set – it should not brown too much or it will dry out.

Slide onto a warm plate, cut into 4 wedges and serve.

If you find some really fresh swordfish at the market, this is a great way of cooking it. It is easy to overcook and make it tough, so follow the timings given below and err on the side of caution – you can always put the fish back on the heat for a moment or two longer if necessary.

seared swordfish
with new potatoes, beans and olives

Brush the swordfish steaks with 1 tablespoon of the oil, season with salt and pepper and set aside.

To make the dressing, put the remaining oil in a bowl, add the lemon juice, sugar, chives and salt and pepper, beat well and set aside.

Cook the potatoes in a saucepan of lightly salted boiling water for 10 minutes, add the beans and cook for a further 3–4 minutes or until just tender. Drain well. Transfer to a bowl, add the olives and half the dressing and toss well.

Cook the swordfish steaks on a preheated barbecue or stove-top grill pan for about 1½ minutes on each side. Let rest in a warm oven for 5 minutes. Sprinkle the swordfish with the remaining dressing and the balsamic vinegar and serve with the warm potato salad.

4 swordfish steaks, 200 g each

7 tablespoons extra virgin olive oil

2 tablespoons freshly squeezed lemon juice

½ teaspoon caster sugar

1 tablespoon fresh chives, scissor-snipped

500 g new potatoes, halved if large

200 g green beans, trimmed

50 g pitted black olives, chopped

sea salt and freshly ground black pepper

1 tablespoon Reduced Balsamic Vinegar, to serve (page 147)

serves 4

This marinade is typical of Japanese cooking and imparts a really fantastic flavour to the fish. Miso is a fermented soybean-based paste, available in Asian stores and some larger supermarkets and food stores. As a guide, the lighter the colour, the sweeter the flavour.

grilled miso cod

3 tablespoons Japanese soy sauce (shoyu)

3 tablespoons sake

3 tablespoons clear honey

2 tablespoons miso paste

6 cod fillets, 200 g each

to serve

pickled ginger

stir-fried baby bok choy

steamed rice

serves 6

Put the soy sauce, sake, honey and miso in a small saucepan and heat gently until smooth. Set aside to cool completely. Pour into a shallow dish, add the cod fillets, cover and let marinate in the refrigerator for at least 4 hours.

Return to room temperature for 1 hour before cooking. Transfer the fillets to a foil-lined grill pan and cook under a preheated grill for 4 minutes on each side, basting halfway through. Let rest for 5 minutes, then serve with pickled ginger, stir-fried bok choy and rice.

In Greece, stifado (or *stifatho*) can refer to a number of things, but essentially it is a thickened stew with tomato and garlic and olive oil. Sometimes made with beef or rabbit, guinea fowl or even quail, it is a handsome dish, easy to prepare and fragrant with herbs. The flambé is an unusual touch – entirely optional, but fun, especially if you use a pleasant, fruity Metaxa brandy. Serve from the dish, accompanied with torn country bread, noodles, rice or even, oddly, with chips.

greek chicken stifado

1.5 kg chicken, whole or quartered, or 4 breast or leg portions

2 tablespoons extra virgin olive oil

10 whole cloves

20 pearl onions or 10 shallots, halved

8–12 canned artichokes, drained

4 garlic cloves, chopped

2 tablespoons white wine vinegar or freshly squeezed lemon juice

6 tablespoons rich tomato purée (double strength)

450 g canned chopped tomatoes

24 black olives, such as Kalamata

a large bunch of fresh or dried rosemary, oregano, thyme, or a mixture

2 tablespoons Greek Metaxa brandy (optional)

freshly ground black pepper

serves 4

Pat the chicken dry with kitchen paper. Heat the olive oil in a large flameproof casserole, add the chicken and sauté for 8–10 minutes, turning it with tongs from time to time.

Push the cloves into some of the onions and add them all to the pan. Add the artichokes, garlic, vinegar or lemon juice, tomato purée, canned tomatoes, olives and black pepper. Tuck in the herb sprigs around the edges.

Bring to the boil and reduce the heat to low. Cover and simmer for 30 minutes for chicken pieces, or about 60 minutes if using a whole bird, or until the chicken is tender and the sauce has reduced and thickened.

Heat the brandy in a warmed ladle and pour it, flaming, over the stifado. Serve immediately.

In a simple dish such as this, quality ingredients are important. Choose an organic or free-range chicken, unwaxed lemons, a good Modena balsamic vinegar and extra virgin olive oil. It really makes a difference.

about 2 kg chicken pieces

3 lemons, cut into wedges

leaves from a large bunch of rosemary

3 red onions

75 g large black olives, about 10–12, pitted

4 tablespoons balsamic vinegar

2 tablespoons extra virgin olive oil

sea salt and freshly ground black pepper

a large roasting tin

serves 4

rosemary and lemon roasted chicken

Trim off any excess fat from the chicken pieces and put them in a large bowl. Add the lemons and rosemary.

Cut the onions in half lengthways, leaving the root end intact. Cut the halves into wedges and add to the chicken.

Add the olives, balsamic vinegar, olive oil and salt and pepper and mix well to coat the chicken with the flavourings.

Cover and let stand at room temperature for 1 hour, or in the refrigerator overnight.

Put the chicken in a large roasting tin, then add the marinade. Cook in a preheated oven at 190°C (375°F) Gas 5 for 30 minutes. Turn the chicken pieces to ensure even cooking and colouring, then cook for a further 30 minutes.

Remove the chicken from the oven. Using a slotted spoon, lift out the chicken, lemons, onions and olives and put them on a serving dish. Skim the cooking juices, discarding the fat. Pour the juices over the chicken and serve hot or at room temperature.

orange and soy glazed duck

This is a great recipe when you are short of time – it is quick to cook and tastes delicious. Serve the duck breasts with your choice of vegetables such as steamed Chinese leaves, bok choy, steamed broccoli or sautéed spinach.

4 duck breast fillets, about 250 g each

freshly squeezed juice of 1 orange

3 tablespoons dark soy sauce

2 tablespoons maple syrup

½ teaspoon Chinese five-spice powder

2 garlic cloves, crushed

freshly ground Szechuan peppercorns or black pepper

to serve

steamed broccoli, bok choy, or sautéed spinach

1 orange, cut into wedges

a roasting tin

serves 4

Using a sharp knife, score the fat on each duck breast crossways several times, then put the breasts in a shallow dish.

Put the orange juice, soy sauce, maple syrup, Chinese five-spice powder, garlic and pepper in a small jug or bowl, mix well, then pour the mixture over the duck fillets. Cover with clingfilm and let marinate in the refrigerator for as long as possible, preferably overnight, but let them return to room temperature for 1 hour before cooking.

Heat a stove-top grill pan until hot, add the duck breasts, skin side down, and sear for 1–2 minutes. Transfer to a roasting tin and add the marinade juices. Cook the duck in a preheated oven at 200°C (400°F) Gas 6 for about 10 minutes or until medium rare. Remove the duck from the oven, wrap it in foil and keep it warm for 5 minutes.

Pour the juices from the roasting tin into a small saucepan and, using a large spoon, very carefully skim the fat off the surface. Heat the juices and boil for 2 minutes, until thickened slightly. Serve the duck breasts sprinkled with the juices and accompanied by broccoli, bok choy or spinach and orange wedges.

This is the best way to cook lamb on the barbecue – the bone is removed and the meat opened out flat so it cooks quickly and evenly.

butterflied lamb
with white bean salad

Put the lamb in a shallow dish, pour over the marinade, cover and let marinate in the refrigerator overnight. Remove from the refrigerator 1 hour before cooking.

To make the salsa verde, put all the ingredients except the oil in a food processor and blend to a smooth paste. With the machine running, gradually pour the oil through the feed tube to form a sauce, then taste and add salt and pepper to taste.

To make the salad, put the onion in a colander, sprinkle with salt and let drain for 30 minutes. Wash the onion in cold water and dry well. Transfer to a bowl and add the beans, garlic, tomatoes, olive oil, vinegar, parsley and salt and pepper to taste.

Preheat the barbecue. Drain the lamb and discard the marinade. Cook over medium-hot coals for 12–15 minutes on each side until charred on the outside but still pink in the middle (cook for a little longer if you prefer the meat less rare). Let the lamb rest for 10 minutes. Cut the lamb into slices and serve with the bean salad and salsa verde.

1.5–2 kg leg of lamb, butterflied (ask your butcher to bone the lamb for you)

1 recipe Herb, Lemon and Garlic Marinade (page 235)

sea salt and freshly ground black pepper

white bean salad

1 large red onion, finely chopped

3 cans haricot beans, about 400 g each, drained

2 garlic cloves, chopped

3 tomatoes, deseeded and chopped

75 ml extra virgin olive oil

1½ tablespoons red wine vinegar

2 tablespoons chopped fresh parsley

salsa verde

a bunch of parsley (about 25 g)

a small bunch of mixed fresh herbs such as basil, chives and mint

1 garlic clove, chopped

1 tablespoon pitted green olives

1 tablespoon capers, drained and washed

2 anchovy fillets, washed and chopped

1 teaspoon Dijon mustard

2 teaspoons white wine vinegar

150 ml extra virgin olive oil

serves 8

souvlaki in pita

4 large pita breads

water and olive oil, to moisten the bread

2 teaspoons chopped fresh oregano, or 1 teaspoon dried oregano, crushed

2 tablespoons freshly squeezed lemon juice

½ onion, coarsely grated

2 tablespoons extra virgin olive oil

500 g lean pork or lamb (usually leg meat), cut into 2 cm cubes

salad, such as

lettuce or cabbage, thinly sliced

cucumber, sliced

red pepper, sliced

tomatoes, cut into wedges

radishes, halved

red onion, sliced into rings

garlic dressing

100 ml thick, strained Greek yoghurt

4 garlic cloves, crushed

5 cm cucumber, coarsely grated, then squeezed dry

½ teaspoon sea salt

metal skewers

serves 4

Souvlaki is the Greek equivalent of the kebab, a street food traditionally eaten at festival time. It is usually made of pork (though lamb is used when in season). Loved by locals and travellers alike, it is filling and delicious.

Brush or sprinkle the pita breads all over with the water and oil and either grill, or bake in a preheated oven at 180°C (350°F) Gas 4 for 3–5 minutes or long enough to soften the bread, but not dry it. Cut off a strip from the long side, then pull open and part the sides of the breads to make a pocket. Push the strip inside. Keep the breads warm.

Put the oregano, lemon juice, grated onion and oil in a bowl and mash with a fork. Add the cubed meat and toss well. Cover and let marinate for 10–20 minutes. Drain, then thread the meat onto metal skewers. Cook on a preheated barbecue or stove-top grill pan, turning occasionally, for 5–8 minutes or until golden outside and cooked through.

Put your choice of salad ingredients in a bowl, toss gently, then insert into the pockets of the pita breads.

To make the dressing, put the yoghurt in a bowl, then beat in the garlic, cucumber and salt. Add a large spoonful to each pocket.

Remove the hot, cooked meat from the skewers, then push it into the pockets. Serve immediately, while the meat and bread are hot and the salad cool.

pasta, pizza & rice

This sauce is best made as soon as the new season's tomatoes arrive in the shops, especially the vine-ripened varieties that we see more and more. If you don't have gas then simply plunge the tomatoes into boiling water for 1 minute, drain, refresh and peel the skin.

pasta with fresh tomato

1 kg ripe tomatoes

6 tablespoons extra virgin olive oil

2 red chillies, deseeded and chopped

2 garlic cloves, crushed

a bunch of basil, chopped

1 teaspoon caster sugar

350 g dried spaghetti

sea salt and cracked black pepper

grated pecorino Sardo or Parmesan cheese, to serve (optional)

serves 4

Holding each tomato with tongs or a skewer, char them over a gas flame until the skins blister and start to shrivel. Peel off the skins, chop the flesh and put in a bowl. Add the oil, chillies, garlic, basil, sugar, salt and pepper and let infuse while you cook the pasta (or longer if possible).

Bring a large saucepan of water to the boil. Add a large pinch of salt, then the pasta and cook for about 10 minutes until *al dente* or according to the timings on the packet. Drain well and immediately stir in the fresh tomato sauce. Serve at once, sprinkled with the grated cheese, if using.

Wide ribbon pasta is particularly popular in Tuscany and also in Umbria. Frequently, it is served with rich meat and game sauces, but freshly made basil oil dressing is a superb summery alternative. Eat this dish on its own or as an accompaniment.

pappardelle with basil oil

350 g dried pappardelle
(wide pasta ribbons),
plain or frilly edged

6 tablespoons extra virgin olive oil

2 garlic cloves, chopped

a handful of fresh chives, chervil,
dill or parsley, plus extra to serve
(optional)

2 large handfuls of fresh
basil leaves

4 tablespoons flaked almonds

4 tablespoons freshly grated
pecorino or Parmesan cheese

sea salt and freshly ground
black pepper

lemon wedges, to serve (optional)

serves 4

Bring a large saucepan of water to the boil. Add a large pinch of salt, then the pappardelle and cook for about 10 minutes until *al dente*, or according to the timings on the packet.

Meanwhile, heat half the oil in a frying pan. Add the garlic, chives and one handful of the basil leaves and sauté for 1–1½ minutes or until the greens have wilted and the garlic is aromatic.

Transfer to a small food processor and blend to a paste. Alternatively, transfer to a mortar and pound with a pestle. Pour into a plastic or stainless steel (non-reactive) sieve set over a bowl. Press all the oil through with the back of a ladle or wooden spoon.

Heat the remaining olive oil in the frying pan, add the almonds and sauté until golden.

Drain the cooked pasta, add it to the frying pan with the almonds, the basil oil and the remaining basil leaves, the cheese and extra chives, if using. Add salt and pepper to taste and toss lightly over the heat. Serve the pasta hot or warm, with lemon wedges, if using.

variation Alternatively, don't strain the basil mixture – just stir it through the cooked pasta and proceed as in the main recipe.

slow-roasted tomatoes
with ricotta and spaghetti

6 large, ripe tomatoes, halved

4 sprigs of oregano, plus
2 tablespoons chopped
fresh oregano

7 tablespoons extra virgin olive oil

500 g spaghetti

4 garlic cloves, sliced

1 dried red chilli, chopped

freshly squeezed juice of ½ lemon

200 g fresh ricotta cheese,
crumbled into big pieces

sea salt and freshly ground
black pepper

freshly grated Parmesan cheese,
to serve

a shallow roasting tin

serves 4

A pasta dish full of the flavours of the Mediterranean. Roast the tomatoes ahead of time if you like and then reheat at 180°C (350°F) Gas 4 for 15 minutes.

Put the tomatoes, cut side up, in a shallow roasting tin. Sprinkle with the sprigs of oregano, 1 tablespoon of the oil and lots of salt and pepper. Roast in a preheated oven at 240°C (475°F) Gas 9 for 20 minutes. Reduce to 150°C (300°F) Gas 2 and cook for a further 1–1½ hours until the tomatoes are golden, glossy and reduced in size by about one-third. Remove from the oven and keep them warm.

Bring a large saucepan of water to the boil. Add a large pinch of salt, then the spaghetti and cook for about 10 minutes until *al dente*, or according to the timings on the packet.

After about 5 minutes, put the remaining oil in a large, deep frying pan, heat well, add the garlic and fry gently for 2 minutes until softened but not golden. Add the chilli and cook for 1 minute more.

Drain the cooked pasta, reserving 4 tablespoons of the cooking liquid. Add the pasta and the reserved cooking liquid to the frying pan, then add the chopped oregano, lemon juice and salt and pepper. Toss over the heat for about 2 minutes.

Serve topped with the roasted tomatoes and ricotta and a light dusting of grated Parmesan.

Of course you can use store-bought fresh pasta, but have a go at making it yourself if you have the time, you really will notice the difference. Try this one flavoured with dill and black pepper – really punchy with rich smoky salmon and the sharpness of lemon butter sauce.

smoked salmon in lemon cream sauce
with dill tagliatelle

To make the pasta, sift the flour and salt onto a board and make a well in the centre. Put the eggs, oil, pepper and dill in a food processor and blend until smooth. Pour into the well in the flour and gradually mix it in, bringing the dough together. Knead for 5–10 minutes until smooth. Wrap the dough, then let rest at room temperature for 30 minutes.

Using a pasta machine, roll the dough into sheets, then cut into tagliatelle – strips about 1 cm wide. Hang up to dry slightly or arrange on clean tea towels dusted with semolina flour.

To make the sauce, put the lemon zest, cream and fish stock in a saucepan, bring to the boil, then remove from the heat and let infuse for 15 minutes. Remove and discard the lemon zest, then boil the sauce rapidly until it has slightly thickened and reduced.

Bring a large saucepan of water to the boil. Add a pinch of salt, then the tagliatelle, stirring well. Return to the boil – when the water is boiling again, the pasta is cooked. Drain well, return it to the pan, add the lemon cream sauce and smoked salmon and toss quickly. Transfer to warm bowls, scatter with more chopped dill and serve immediately.

250 g smoked salmon, cut into strips

sea salt

chopped dill, to serve

fresh pasta

300 g strong white bread flour

½ teaspoon salt

3 eggs

1 tablespoon olive oil

1 tablespoon freshly ground black pepper (very finely ground)

50 g fresh dill sprigs

fine semolina flour, for dusting (optional)

lemon cream sauce

zest of 2 unwaxed lemons

300 ml double cream

150 ml well-flavoured fish stock

a pasta machine

serves 4

chilli tuna tartare pasta

'Tartare' means uncooked and, to serve fish this way, you must use very fresh, sashimi-grade tuna. If you prefer your tuna cooked, sear it on a preheated stove-top grill pan for 1 minute on each side or until cooked to your liking. However, do try it tartare – it is delicious, as the Japanese well know.

350 g dried fusilli or other pasta

6 tablespoons extra virgin olive oil, plus extra for serving

4 garlic cloves, sliced

1–2 dried red chillies, deseeded and chopped

grated zest and juice of 1 unwaxed lemon

1 tablespoon chopped fresh thyme leaves

500 g tuna steak, chopped

a handful of fresh basil leaves

sea salt and freshly ground black pepper

serves 4

Bring a large saucepan of water to the boil. Add a large pinch of salt, then the pasta and cook for about 10 minutes until *al dente*, or according to the timings on the packet.

Meanwhile, heat the oil in a frying pan, add the garlic and fry gently for 2 minutes until lightly golden. Add the chilli, lemon zest and thyme and fry for a further 1 minute.

Drain the pasta, reserving 4 tablespoons of the cooking liquid, and return both to the pan. Stir in the hot garlic oil mixture, lemon juice, raw tuna, basil leaves, salt and pepper and a little extra olive oil. Serve immediately.

Vary the seafood depending on what's available and best on the day, but always include clams or mussels – for their flavour as well as their beautiful shells.

seafood spaghettini

300 g dried pasta, such as spaghettini

4–5 tablespoons olive oil

1 garlic clove, finely chopped

300 g mixed seafood, such as squid, cut into rings, shelled prawns and scallops, shelled and halved crossways

500 g fresh mussels or clams in shells, scrubbed

2 tablespoons chopped fresh flat leaf parsley

sea salt and freshly ground black pepper

serves 4

Bring a large saucepan of water to the boil. Add a large pinch of salt, then the spaghettini and cook for about 10 minutes until *al dente* or according to the timings on the packet.

Meanwhile, heat half the oil in a large sauté pan or saucepan. Add the mixed seafood and cook for 3–4 minutes, stirring constantly until just cooked. Transfer to a large bowl and set aside.

Add the mussels or clams to the pan, cover with a lid and cook for 5 minutes until all the shells have opened, discarding any that remain closed.

Drain the pasta and return it to the warm pan. Add the mussels or clams, seafood, remaining olive oil and parsley. Add salt and pepper to taste, toss gently to mix, then serve immediately.

This is similar to the Italian 'calzone' or stuffed pizza. They are often available at Turkish food stalls, where the chefs busily knead, roll and cook these delicious pizzas.

turkish pizza turnover

350 g strong white bread flour, plus extra for kneading

1½ teaspoons easy-blend dried yeast

1½ teaspoons sea salt

1 tablespoon extra virgin olive oil

filling

500 g spinach leaves

1 tablespoon extra virgin olive oil

1 small onion, finely chopped

2 garlic cloves, crushed

125 g feta cheese, crumbled

2 tablespoons grated Parmesan cheese

2 tablespoons mascarpone cheese

a little grated nutmeg

freshly ground black pepper

serves 4

Sift the flour into the bowl of an electric mixer with a dough hook attachment. Alternatively, use a food processor with a plastic blade attachment. Stir in the yeast and salt. Add the oil and 150–175 ml warm water and work until the dough is smooth and elastic.

Meanwhile, to make the filling, discard any thick spinach stalks, then wash the leaves in a colander. Drain, transfer to a large saucepan and heat gently for 2–3 minutes until the leaves have wilted. Rinse under cold water, drain completely and squeeze out as much water as possible. Finely chop the spinach and set aside.

Heat the oil in a frying pan, add the onion and garlic and fry gently for 5 minutes until very soft and lightly golden. Stir in the spinach, the cheeses, nutmeg and pepper, then remove from the heat.

Transfer the dough to a lightly floured work surface and knead it gently. Divide the dough into 4 pieces and roll out each one to a rectangle 20 x 40 cm (it will be very thin). Spread a quarter of the spinach mixture over one half of one piece of dough, fold over and seal the edges. Repeat with the other pieces of dough to make 4 turnovers.

Heat the flat plate of a barbecue for 5 minutes, then reduce the heat to medium. Brush with a little oil, add the stuffed pizzas and cook for 4–5 minutes on each side until golden. Alternatively, cook on a flat griddle or large, heavy-based frying pan. Serve hot.

If you haven't got a pizza stone or flat earthenware tile to bake the pizza on, use a heavy, old, dark, baking sheet instead.

500 g strong white bread flour, plus extra for kneading

2 tablespoons sugar

1½ teaspoons salt

1 sachet micronized fast-acting yeast, 7 g

300 ml lukewarm water

1 egg, beaten

2 tablespoons extra virgin olive oil

topping

400 g canned chopped plum tomatoes

2 garlic cloves, chopped

1 tablespoon sugar

4 tablespoons extra virgin olive oil

a large handful of fresh basil leaves, torn

24 anchovy fillets

24 capers

1 dried red chilli, crumbled (optional)

200 g mozzarella cheese, sliced (optional)

24 black olives, pitted

1 pizza stone or baking sheet

a pizza peel

makes 4

pizza napoletana

Put the flour, sugar, salt and yeast in a food processor. Pulse a few times to mix and sift. Put the warm water, egg and olive oil in a bowl or jug and whisk well. With the machine running, add the mixture to the processor through the feed tube. The dough will form, clump, then gather in a mass. Remove to a well-floured work surface, sprinkle with extra flour and knead the dough for 2–3 minutes or until smooth and silky.

Put the dough in a lightly oiled bowl and enclose in a plastic bag. Leave in a warm place until doubled in size, about 1 hour. Remove the dough from the bowl and punch it down. Cut into 4 equal pieces. Preheat the pizza stone or baking sheet at 220°C (425°F) Gas 7 until very hot.

Put the pieces of dough on a well-floured work surface and shape into rounds 1 cm thick, but thicker around the edges. Make indentations with your fingertips all over the surface. Let rise while you make the topping.

Meanwhile, put the tomatoes in a large, shallow saucepan and add the garlic, sugar, half the oil and half the basil. Bring to the boil and cook, uncovered, for 8–12 minutes until reduced by half. Use a peel to slide one pizza dough base onto the hot pizza stone or baking sheet. Spread one-quarter of the hot tomato sauce on top leaving 3 cm bare at the edges. Sprinkle with one-quarter of the anchovies, capers, and chilli and mozzarella, if using. Return to the oven and bake for 10–12 minutes or until risen, blistered, hot and fragrant. Top with a few basil leaves, a little oil and serve hot or warm. Repeat to make 3 more.

This delicious Spanish tart, or coca, can be found in tapas bars. Piled hot and high and served with olives and glasses of local wine, it can be a revelation. If you haven't any piquillo peppers, use canned pimiento or grilled or roasted fresh red peppers.

spanish tart with peppers

To make the dough, put the flour, yeast and salt in a bowl and mix. Add the water and mix to a satiny dough, then knead, still in the bowl for 5 minutes or until silky. Cover the bowl with a cloth and leave for about 1 hour or until the dough has doubled in size.

Meanwhile, to make the topping, heat 3 tablespoons of the oil in a frying pan, add the onions and cook, stirring over medium heat until softened and transparent. Slice half the piquillos and add to the pan. Stir in most of the herbs.

Transfer the dough to a heavy, dark, oiled baking sheet. Punch down, flatten and roll out the dough to a circle 30 cm diameter. Snip, twist or roll the edges. Spread the anchovy paste all over the top. Add the remaining piquillos, left whole, and the cooked onion mixture. Arrange the anchovies and remaining herbs in a decorative pattern on top and sprinkle with the remaining oil.

Bake in a preheated oven at 220°C (425°F) Gas 7 for 25–30 minutes until the base is crisp and risen, the edges golden and the filling hot and wilted. Serve in wedges, hot or cool.

250 g plain white flour

½ sachet micronized fast-acting yeast, 3.5 g

½ teaspoon salt

150 ml lukewarm water

topping

4 tablespoons extra virgin olive oil

350 g red onions, cut into wedges

about 500 g canned piquillo peppers, drained

leaves from a small handful of fresh thyme or rosemary sprigs

2 tablespoons anchovy paste or purée, or canned anchovies, chopped and mashed

16 marinated anchovy fillets

a baking sheet, oiled

serves 4–6

Although this risotto is best made with fresh peas, you can also use frozen ones. The mint adds a delicious fresh flavour. This will serve four people as a main course or six as a starter.

fresh pea and lettuce risotto

50 g butter

1 large onion, finely chopped

2 garlic cloves, crushed

1 leek, trimmed and sliced

300 g arborio rice

150 ml dry vermouth or fino sherry

1 litre vegetable stock

350 g fresh or frozen peas

125 g cos lettuce leaves, washed and shredded

4 tablespoons chopped fresh mint leaves, plus extra leaves, to serve

50 g mascarpone cheese

75 g freshly grated Parmesan cheese

sea salt and freshly ground black pepper

serves 4–6

Put the butter in a saucepan, melt gently, then add the onion, garlic and leek and fry gently for 10 minutes until softened but not golden. Add the rice, stir for 1 minute until all the grains are glossy, then add the vermouth or sherry. Let bubble and evaporate.

Meanwhile, put the stock in a separate saucepan and heat until just barely simmering. Add about 150 ml of the stock to the rice. Add the peas and a little salt and pepper, then stir until the liquid has been absorbed. Continue adding the stock and stirring the rice until almost all the stock has been used. Add the lettuce, chopped mint and the remaining stock and cook until absorbed.

Remove the pan from the heat, stir in the mascarpone and 50 g of the Parmesan and season to taste with salt and pepper. Cover the pan and set aside for 5 minutes before serving, topped with the remaining Parmesan and mint leaves.

paella

8 chicken drumsticks and thighs, mixed, or 1 whole chicken, about 1.5 kg, cut into pieces

2 teaspoons sea salt

4 teaspoons smoked paprika or paprika

4 tablespoons extra virgin olive oil

3–4 boneless pork chops, or 325 g salt pork cut into 3 cm cubes

2 onions, chopped

4 garlic cloves, crushed

500 g tomatoes, fresh or canned, skinned, deseeded and chopped

2 large pinches of saffron threads, or 3 sachets ground saffron

350 g calasparra (paella) rice

750–800 ml boiling chicken stock or water

100 g shelled fresh peas, or frozen peas, thawed

200 g green beans, halved

8 baby artichokes, halved lengthways, or canned or marinated equivalent

8 large uncooked prawns, shell on

freshly ground black pepper

serves 4–6

This now-grand Spanish rice dish, once a poor man's food from Albufera in Valencia, is made in countless variations in different areas, depending on local ingredients and styles. Use hard, stubby, calasparra rice (sometimes labelled 'paella rice' in supermarkets) and don't stir it constantly like risotto.

Pat the chicken dry with kitchen paper. Put the salt, pepper and paprika in a bowl and mix well. Sprinkle the chicken with half the mixture and toss well.

Heat the oil in a large, shallow frying pan. Add the chicken and pork, in batches if necessary, and sauté over medium heat for 10–12 minutes or until well browned. Remove with a slotted spoon and set aside.

Add the onions, garlic, tomatoes and saffron to the pan, then add the remaining salt and paprika mixture. Cook until thickened, about 5 minutes. Stir well, then return the meats to the pan, stir in the rice and most of the hot stock. Cook over high heat until bubbling fiercely, then reduce the heat and simmer gently, uncovered, for 15 minutes.

Add the peas, beans, artichokes, prawns and remaining stock, if necessary, and continue to cook for 10–15 minutes or until the rice is cooked and glossy but dry. Serve the paella straight from the pan.

barbecue

Serving a large platter of grilled vegetables provides a
lovely start to any barbecue – just choose a combination of
your favourites. A delicious way to serve them is on a bed
of grilled polenta.

vegetable antipasto

2 red peppers

4 baby fennel bulbs

1 large aubergine

2 large courgettes

1 red onion

1 recipe Herb, Lemon and
Garlic Marinade (page 235)

a few fresh herb leaves,
such as basil, dill, fennel,
mint and parsley

extra virgin olive oil, to taste

freshly squeezed lemon juice,
to taste

sea salt and freshly ground
black pepper

bread or grilled polenta, to serve

serves 4

Cut the peppers into quarters and remove and discard the seeds.
Trim the fennel, reserving the fronds, and cut the bulbs into 5 mm
slices. Cut the aubergine into thick slices and cut in half again.
Cut the courgettes into thick slices diagonally and cut the onion
into wedges.

Put all the vegetables in a large bowl, add the marinade and toss
gently until evenly coated. Cover and let marinate in a cool place
for at least 1 hour.

Preheat the barbecue, then cook all the vegetables on the grill
rack, turning occasionally, until they are tender and lightly charred.
Let cool, then peel the peppers.

Arrange the vegetables on a large platter, sprinkle with the herbs,
reserved fennel fronds, olive oil and lemon juice, then season
lightly with salt and pepper.

Serve at room temperature with crusty bread or grilled polenta.

The nut sauce, tarator, served with these leeks is found in Middle Eastern cooking, though cooks there would use ground almonds or walnuts. If the sauce is made in advance, whisk well before use.

charred leeks with tarator sauce

750 g baby leeks, trimmed

2–3 tablespoons extra virgin olive oil

sea salt

lemon wedges, to serve

tarator sauce

50 g macadamia nuts, toasted

25 g fresh breadcrumbs

2 garlic cloves, crushed

100 ml extra virgin olive oil

1 tablespoon freshly squeezed lemon juice

2 tablespoons boiling water

freshly ground black pepper

serves 4

To make the sauce, put the nuts in a food processor and grind coarsely, then add the breadcrumbs and garlic and process again to form a smooth paste. Transfer to a bowl and very gradually whisk in the olive oil, lemon juice and the 2 tablespoons boiling water to form a sauce. Season to taste with salt and pepper.

Preheat the barbecue. Brush the leeks with a little olive oil, season with salt and cook over medium-hot coals for 6–10 minutes, turning occasionally, until charred and tender. Transfer to a serving plate, sprinkle with the remaining olive oil, then pour the sauce over the top. Serve with lemon wedges.

400 g canned corn kernels, drained

65 g polenta

50 g plain flour

1 teaspoon baking powder

½ teaspoon bicarbonate of soda

½ teaspoon salt

150 ml buttermilk

1 tablespoon vegetable oil

½ large free range egg

olive oil, for spraying

to serve

smoked salmon

crème fraîche

salmon caviar

serves 4

To cook these delicious cakes you will need a barbecue with a flat plate. Alternatively, you can use a flat griddle or heavy-based frying pan preheated over the hot coals. Either way, they taste absolutely wonderful.

sweetcorn griddle cakes

Put half the corn in a food processor and blend until fairly smooth. Add the polenta, flour, baking powder, bicarbonate of soda, salt, buttermilk, vegetable oil and egg and blend to form a thick batter. Transfer to a bowl and stir in the remaining corn.

Preheat the flat plate on your barbecue to low and spray with olive oil. Spoon on the batter to make 4 cakes, 10 cm diameter and cook for 2 minutes. Using a spatula, flip the cakes over and cook for a further 30 seconds or until golden on both sides and firm to the touch. If you don't have a flat plate, use a heavy flat griddle or frying pan, either on the barbecue, or on the stove. Transfer to a plate and keep the corn cakes warm.

Repeat to make 8 cakes. Serve, topped with smoked salmon, crème fraîche and salmon caviar.

Coating the prawns with sea salt protects the flesh during cooking so that when you shell them, the meat inside is sweet and moist.

salt-crusted prawns
with tomato, avocado and olive salad

20 large uncooked prawns

1 tablespoon extra virgin olive oil

3 tablespoons sea salt

tomato, avocado and olive salad

4–6 large ripe tomatoes, sliced

1 large ripe avocado, halved, stoned and sliced

50 g pitted black olives

a handful of fresh mint leaves

4 tablespoons extra virgin olive oil

1 tablespoon reduced balsamic vinegar*

shavings of fresh Parmesan cheese

sea salt and freshly ground black pepper

serves 4

To prepare the salad, put the tomatoes and avocado on a plate with the olives and mint leaves. Put the olive oil and vinegar in a jug and stir well, then pour over the salad. Scatter the Parmesan shavings over the top and season with salt and pepper to taste.

Using kitchen scissors, cut down the back of each prawn to reveal the intestinal vein. Pull it out and discard, but leave the shell on. Wash the prawns under cold running water, pat dry with kitchen paper and transfer to a bowl. Sprinkle over the olive oil and toss well. Put the salt onto a plate and use to coat the prawns.

Preheat the barbecue, then cook the prawns over hot coals for 2–3 minutes on each side until cooked through. Let cool slightly, peel off the shells, then serve with the tomato, avocado and olive salad.

note To reduce balsamic vinegar, put 300 ml in a saucepan and boil gently until it has reduced by about two-thirds and has reached the consistency of thick syrup. Let cool, then store in a clean jar or bottle.

Whole scallops grilled on the half shell look just great. If you can't find any with shells, don't despair, simply thread whole scallops onto soaked wooden skewers, brush with the melted butter mixture and grill for 1 minute on each side. Serve, sprinkled with the remaining butter and coriander.

scallops with lemongrass and lime butter

2 stalks of lemongrass

grated zest and juice of ½ large unwaxed lime

100 g butter, softened

1 small fresh red chilli, deseeded and finely chopped

1 tablespoon Thai fish sauce

24 scallops on the half shell

1 tablespoon chopped fresh coriander

freshly ground black pepper

serves 4

Using a sharp knife, trim the lemongrass stalks to about 15 cm, then remove the tough outer leaves. Chop the inner stalk very thinly and put in a saucepan with the lime zest and juice, butter, chilli and fish sauce. Heat gently until the butter has melted, then simmer for 1 minute. Remove from the heat and let cool.

Remove and discard the corals from the scallops and make sure the meat is not still attached to the shell. If it is, carefully cut through the muscle to release the scallop. Leave the scallops on the shells and spoon a little of the butter mixture over each one.

Preheat the barbecue, then put the shells on the grill rack and cook for 3–4 minutes, turning the scallops over halfway through with tongs. Serve at once sprinkled with chopped coriander and freshly ground black pepper.

This is a great way to cook clams on the barbecue,
where all the wonderful juices are collected in the
foil parcel. Mop them up with plenty of crusty bread.

clam parcels with garlic butter

1 kg vongole clams

125 g unsalted butter, softened

grated zest and juice of
½ unwaxed lemon

2 garlic cloves, crushed

2 tablespoons chopped
fresh parsley

freshly ground black pepper

crusty bread, to serve

serves 4

Wash the clams under cold running water and scrub the
shells. Discard any with broken shells or any that don't
close when tapped lightly with a knife. Shake the clams
dry and divide among 4 pieces of foil.

Put the butter, lemon zest and juice, garlic, parsley and
pepper in a bowl and beat well, then divide equally
among the 4 piles of clams. Wrap the foil over the clams
and seal the edges to form parcels.

Preheat the barbecue, then put the parcels on the grill
rack and cook for 5 minutes. Check one parcel to see if
the clams have opened and serve if ready or cook a little
longer, if needed. Serve with crusty bread.

A great way to prepare whole salmon is to remove the central bone from the fish, then tie the two fillets back together. If your filleting skills are limited, just ask your fishmonger to fillet the whole fish for you.

whole salmon stuffed with herbs

Put the salmon fillets flat on a board, flesh side up. Carefully pull out any remaining bones with tweezers.

Put the butter, herbs, lemon zest, garlic and plenty of pepper in a small bowl and beat well. Spread the mixture over one of the salmon fillets and put the second on top, arranging them top to tail.

Using kitchen string, tie the fish together at 2.5 cm intervals. Brush with a little oil, sprinkle with salt and freshly ground black pepper and cook on the flat plate of a barbecue for 10 minutes on each side. Alternatively, use a stove-top grill pan or a large, heavy-based frying pan.

Let rest for 10 minutes, then remove the string and serve the fish cut into portions.

2 kg whole salmon, filleted

125 g butter, softened

25 g chopped, fresh soft-leaf mixed herbs, such as basil, chives, mint, parsley and tarragon

grated zest of 1 unwaxed lemon

1 garlic clove, crushed

olive oil, for brushing

sea salt and freshly ground black pepper

serves 8

This is a typical Greek dish of char-grilled bream with oil, oregano and garlic. If you can't find bream, use other small fish such as red mullet, snapper or even trout.

barbecued fish
bathed in oregano and lemon

2 unwaxed lemons

250 ml extra virgin olive oil

1 tablespoon dried oregano

2 garlic cloves, finely chopped

2 tablespoons chopped fresh flat leaf parsley

6 bream or snapper, about 350 g each, well cleaned and scaled

sea salt and freshly ground black pepper

serves 6

Grate the zest of 1 lemon into a small bowl and squeeze in the juice. Add 225 ml of the oil, the oregano, garlic, parsley, salt and pepper. Cover and let infuse for at least 1 hour.

Wash and dry the fish inside and out. Using a sharp knife, cut several slashes into each side. Squeeze the juice from the remaining lemon into a bowl, add the remaining 4 tablespoons of oil, salt and pepper and rub the mixture all over the fish.

Heat the flat plate of your barbecue for 10 minutes, add the fish and cook for 3–4 minutes on each side until charred and cooked through. Alternatively, use a large, heavy-based frying pan or stove-top grill pan. Transfer the fish to a large, warm platter, pour over the oregano dressing and let rest for 5 minutes before serving.

Panini, which is Italian for toasted sandwiches, can be prepared ahead of time, then cooked just before you want to serve them. The combination of char-grilled peppers, tender chicken and a delicious rocket aïoli is definitely hard to beat.

chicken panini with roasted pepper and rocket aïoli

Preheat the barbecue, then cook the peppers over hot coals or grill them for about 20 minutes until charred all over. Put them in a plastic bag and let cool. Peel off the skin, cut the peppers in half, remove and discard the seeds, then cut the flesh into strips.

To make the aïoli, put the egg yolk, vinegar and a little salt and pepper in a food processor and blend briefly until frothy. Add the rocket and garlic and pulse for 30 seconds. With the machine still running, gradually pour in the olive oil through the feed tube until the sauce is thickened and speckled with vivid green. Taste and add more salt and pepper, if necessary.

Spread a little of the rocket aïoli onto the cut sides of each roll and fill the rolls with the chicken, pepper strips and spinach leaves. Press the halves together.

Preheat the flat plate on the barbecue and cook the panini over low heat for 4–5 minutes on each side until toasted. If you don't have a flat plate, cook on a stove-top grill pan. Serve hot.

2 red peppers

4 small focaccia or Turkish rolls, halved

2 large, cooked chicken breasts, shredded

a small handful of baby spinach

rocket aïoli

1 egg yolk

1 teaspoon white wine vinegar

a bunch of rocket, about 50 g, coarsely chopped

1 garlic clove, crushed

150 ml olive oil

sea salt and freshly ground black pepper

serves 4

Jerk seasoning is Jamaica's popular spice mix, used to spark up meat, poultry and fish, especially the delicious barbecued offerings sold at the roadside jerk huts. The seasoning is a combination of allspice, cinnamon, chilli, nutmeg, thyme and sugar and is available in powder or paste form from larger supermarkets and specialist food stores.*

12 chicken wings

2 tablespoons extra virgin olive oil

1 tablespoon jerk seasoning powder or 2 tablespoons paste

freshly squeezed juice of ½ lemon

1 teaspoon sea salt

avocado salsa

1 large ripe avocado

2 ripe tomatoes, peeled, deseeded and chopped

1 garlic clove, crushed

1 small red chilli, deseeded and chopped

freshly squeezed juice of ½ lemon

2 tablespoons chopped fresh coriander

1 tablespoon extra virgin olive oil

sea salt and freshly ground black pepper

serves 4

jerk chicken wings
with avocado salsa

Put the chicken wings in a ceramic dish. Mix the oil, jerk seasoning, lemon juice and salt in a bowl, pour it over the wings and stir well until evenly coated. Cover and let marinate overnight in the refrigerator.

The next day, cook the wings either on a barbecue or under a hot grill for 5–6 minutes each side, basting occasionally with any remaining marinade until charred and tender.

Meanwhile, to make the salsa, put all the ingredients in a bowl, mix well and season to taste with salt and pepper. Serve the wings with the salsa.

*note If you don't have any jerk seasoning on hand, try another spice mix or spice paste instead. Just remember, jerk is very fiery indeed, so you need a spicy one.

chicken skewers
with thyme and sesame

This spice dip, called *zahtar*, is served with pita bread. It is sold ready-made from Middle Eastern stores, but it is very easy to make your own.

3 tablespoons extra virgin olive oil

750 g boneless chicken breast fillets, cut into bite-sized pieces

zahtar spice mix

3 tablespoons sesame seeds, toasted

30 g fresh thyme leaves

½ teaspoon sea salt

to serve

chilli oil

freshly squeezed juice of 1–2 lemons

mixed salad leaves

8 wooden skewers soaked in cold water for 30 minutes

serves 4

To make the zahtar spice mix, put the sesame seeds in a dry frying pan and toast over medium heat until golden and aromatic. Remove the pan from the heat, let cool, then transfer to a spice grinder (or clean coffee grinder). Add the thyme and salt, then blend to a coarse powder. Alternatively, use a mortar and pestle. You will need 3 tablespoons for this recipe (put the remainder in an airtight container and keep in a cool place for future use).

Put the 3 tablespoons zahtar spice mix in a shallow dish, add the olive oil and mix. well Add the chicken pieces and toss well until coated. Cover and let marinate in the refrigerator for at least 2 hours.

Preheat the barbecue, then thread the chicken pieces onto the soaked wooden skewers and cook over hot coals for 2–3 minutes on each side. Remove from the heat, let rest briefly, sprinkle with chilli oil and lemon juice and serve hot with salad leaves.

barbecued mexican-style poussins

To make the salsa, preheat a grill until hot. Add the corn and cook for about 15 minutes, turning frequently, until charred on all sides. Let cool. Next, grill the chillies until the skins are charred all over. Transfer to a bowl and cover with a clean cloth until cool. Using a sharp knife, cut down all sides of the corn cob to remove the kernels. Put them in a bowl. Peel and deseed the chillies, chop the flesh and add it to the corn. Stir in all the remaining salsa ingredients, then season to taste with salt and pepper.

To spatchcock the poussins, turn them breast side down and, using poultry shears or sturdy scissors, cut down each side of the backbone and discard it. Turn the birds over and open them out flat, pressing down hard on the breastbone. Thread 2 skewers diagonally through each bird from the wings to the thigh bones.

To make the marinade, skewer the chillies and garlic together and cook under a medium-hot grill for 10 minutes, turning frequently, until evenly browned. Scrape off and discard the skins from the chillies and chop the flesh. Put the flesh and seeds in a food processor, add the garlic and all the remaining marinade ingredients and blend to a purée.

Pour the marinade over the poussins and let marinate in the refrigerator overnight. Return them to room temperature for 1 hour before cooking. Remove the birds from the marinade and barbecue over medium-hot coals for 12 minutes on each side, basting occasionally. Let rest for 5 minutes. Serve with the salsa.

4 poussins

mexican marinade

4 jalapeño chillies

8 garlic cloves, peeled

4 tablespoons freshly squeezed orange juice

2 tablespoons freshly squeezed lime juice

1 tablespoon ground cumin

1 tablespoon dried oregano or thyme

2 teaspoons sea salt

6 tablespoons olive oil

1 tablespoon maple syrup or clear honey

creamy corn salsa

1 ear of fresh corn, husk removed

2 red chillies

1 tomato, diced

1 garlic clove, crushed

freshly squeezed juice of ½ lime

1 tablespoon maple syrup

2 tablespoons sour cream

sea salt and freshly ground black pepper

8 metal skewers

serves 4

lamb burgers
with mint yoghurt

A good burger should be thick, moist, tender and juicy. These lamb burgers are all that and more. Serve in crusty rolls with a few slices of tomato, plenty of salad leaves and a generous spoonful of the minty yoghurt dressing. The perfect burger for a barbecue party.

Put the lamb and pork in a food processor and process briefly until coarsely ground. Transfer to a bowl and, using your hands, work in the chopped onion, garlic, cumin, cinnamon, oregano, salt, breadcrumbs, capers, beaten egg and pepper. Cover and let marinate in the refrigerator for at least 2 hours.

To make the mint yoghurt, put the yoghurt in a bowl and stir in the mint and a little salt and pepper to taste.

Using damp hands, shape the meat into 8 patties. Preheat the barbecue, then brush the grill rack with oil. Cook the patties for about 3 minutes on each side.

Split the rolls in half, add a cooked patty, salad leaves, tomato slices and a spoonful of the mint yoghurt. Serve immediately.

variation For a traditional hamburger, replace the lamb with beef, omit the spices and, instead of the capers, add 4 chopped anchovy fillets. Serve in burger buns with salad.

650 g boneless lamb shoulder, cut into 2 cm cubes

100 g pork belly, chopped

1 onion, very finely chopped

2 garlic cloves, crushed

2 tablespoon ground cumin

2 teaspoons ground cinnamon

1 tablespoon dried oregano

2 teaspoons sea salt

50 g fresh breadcrumbs

1 tablespoon capers, drained and chopped

1 large free-range egg, beaten

freshly ground black pepper

mint yoghurt

200 g thick yoghurt

2 tablespoons chopped fresh mint leaves

sea salt and freshly ground black pepper

to serve

4 crusty rolls

salad leaves

tomato slices

serves 4

lamb kebabs
with warm chickpea salad

750 g lamb fillet or boneless
leg of lamb, cut into
bite-sized pieces

1 recipe Minted Yoghurt Marinade
(page 235)

warm chickpea salad

150 g dried chickpeas, soaked
overnight in cold water,
drained and rinsed

1 bay leaf

½ onion

6 tablespoons extra virgin olive
oil, plus extra to serve

1 garlic clove, finely chopped

freshly squeezed juice
of ½ lemon

a handful of fresh parsley

a pinch of sweet paprika

sea salt and freshly ground
black pepper

4 metal skewers

serves 4

Pieces of tender lamb, marinated in mint and yoghurt complement the warm chickpeas perfectly. Serve this as part of a Middle Eastern spread with Hoummus (page 179) and Flatbreads (page 184).

Put the pieces of lamb in a shallow dish. Add the marinade and stir well to coat. Cover and let marinate in the refrigerator for 2–4 hours.

Prepare the chickpea salad 1 hour before barbecuing. Put the soaked chickpeas, bay leaf and onion in a heavy-based saucepan and cover with cold water. Bring to the boil and simmer for 45 minutes or until the chickpeas are tender, skimming off the foam from time to time.

Drain the chickpeas and transfer to a bowl. Remove and discard the onion and bay leaf. Mash the chickpeas coarsely with a fork. Stir in the olive oil, garlic, lemon juice, parsley, paprika and salt and pepper to taste.

Meanwhile, preheat the barbecue. Thread the lamb onto the skewers, then cook the kebabs over hot coals for 6–8 minutes, turning halfway through until tender. Serve the kebabs on a bed of chickpea salad, sprinkled with a little extra olive oil.

*2 racks barbecue pork spareribs,
500 g each*

chilli spiked cornbread

150 g medium cornmeal

150 g plain flour

1½ teaspoons sea salt

1 tablespoon baking powder

2 eggs, beaten

250 ml milk

2 tablespoons olive oil

*200 g canned corn kernels,
drained*

*2 large red chillies, deseeded
and chopped*

25 g finely grated Cheddar cheese

*2 tablespoons chopped
fresh coriander*

sweet chilli marinade

2 garlic cloves, crushed

2 tablespoons sea salt

2 tablespoons ground cumin

2 teaspoons chilli powder

1 teaspoon dried oregano

*8 tablespoons maple syrup
or golden syrup*

4 tablespoons red wine vinegar

4 tablespoons olive oil

*a cake tin, 20 cm square,
greased and base-lined
with baking parchment*

serves 4–6

Nibbling away at succulent grilled pork ribs is one of the true pleasures of a barbecue (providing of course you eat meat). Here they are cooked in a marinade of spices and maple syrup giving them the authentic flavour of the American deep south.

tex-mex pork rack

To make the cornbread, put the cornmeal, flour, salt and baking powder in a bowl and mix. Make a well in the centre and pour in the eggs, milk and olive oil. Beat with a wooden spoon to make a smooth batter. Fold in the corn, chillies, cheese and coriander, then spoon into the cake tin. Bake in a preheated oven at 200°C (400°F) Gas 6 for 25 minutes, or until a skewer inserted in the centre comes out clean.

Remove from the oven and let cool in the tin for 5 minutes, then turn out onto a wire rack to cool completely.

Wash the ribs and pat them dry with kitchen paper. Transfer to a shallow, non-metal dish. Put all the marinade ingredients in a bowl, mix well, pour over the ribs, then work in well with your hands. Cover and let marinate overnight in the refrigerator.

The next day, return the ribs to room temperature for 1 hour, then cook on a preheated medium-hot barbecue for 30 minutes, turning and basting frequently with the juices. Let cool a little, then serve with the cornbread.

Don't overcook pork or it will be dry and tough. A good
test is to pierce the meat with a skewer, leave it there
for a second, remove it and carefully feel how hot it is –
it should feel warm, not too hot or too cold.

sage-rubbed pork chops

2 tablespoons chopped
fresh sage leaves

2 tablespoons
wholegrain mustard

2 tablespoons extra
virgin olive oil

4 large pork chops

sea salt and freshly
ground black pepper

**smoky tomato
salsa**

4 ripe plum tomatoes

2 large fresh red chillies

4 garlic cloves, peeled

1 red onion, quartered

4 tablespoons extra
virgin olive oil

1 tablespoon freshly
squeezed lemon juice

2 tablespoons chopped
fresh coriander

2 wooden skewers,
soaked in cold water for
30 minutes

serves 4

Put the sage, mustard and olive oil in a bowl and mix well.
Season with a little salt and pepper, then spread the
mixture all over the chops. Cover and let marinate in the
refrigerator for 1 hour.

Meanwhile, preheat the barbecue. To make the salsa, hold
the tomatoes over the flames of the barbecue with tongs
for about 1 minute, turning frequently, until the skin is
charred all over. Let cool, peel, cut in half and remove and
discard the seeds. Chop the flesh. Repeat with the chillies.

Thread the garlic cloves and onion quarters onto separate
skewers. Cook the garlic over hot coals for 5–6 minutes
and the onion for 10–12 minutes, turning frequently, until
they are charred and softened. Let cool, remove from the
skewers and cut into cubes.

Put the tomatoes, chillies, garlic and onion in a bowl and
stir in the oil, lemon juice and coriander. Season to taste
with salt and pepper.

Cook the chops over hot coals for 2½–3 minutes on each
side until browned and cooked through. Serve hot with
the smoky tomato salsa.

Choosing the right cut of beef for barbecue cooking is the first step to producing the perfect steak. There are several you can use, such as fillet, T-bone or sirloin, but this recipe suggests using rib eye steak. As the name suggests, it is the 'eye' of the rib roast and is marbled with fat, giving a moist result. It has a good flavour and is not too huge.

rib eye steak with anchovy butter

Put the butter, anchovies, parsley and a little pepper in a bowl and beat well. Transfer to a sheet of foil and roll up into a log. Chill in the refrigerator until required.

Preheat the barbecue to high and brush the grill rack with oil. Season the steaks with salt and pepper and cook for 3 minutes on each side for rare, 4–5 minutes for medium and 5–6 minutes for well done.

Transfer the steaks to a warmed serving plate and put 2 slices of anchovy butter on each one. Let rest for about 5 minutes before serving in order to set the juices.

125 g butter, softened

8 anchovy fillets in oil, drained and chopped coarsely

2 tablespoons chopped fresh parsley

4 rib eye steaks, about 250 g each

oil, for brushing

sea salt and freshly ground black pepper

serves 4

dips & breads

400 g dried skinned fava beans

1 fresh bouquet garni of parsley, celery, bay leaf and thyme

1 large onion, coarsely chopped

1 potato, unpeeled

4 garlic cloves, chopped

60 ml extra virgin olive oil, plus extra to serve (optional)

freshly squeezed juice of 1 lemon

6 sprigs of oregano, chopped

sea salt and freshly ground black pepper

to serve

your choice of:
baby leafy vegetables
radishes
cucumber
crusty bread, toasted

serves 4

All around the Mediterranean, fresh and dried peas, beans and lentils are used in dips and spreads, as sauces with pasta and in soups. Depending on the region and local herbs, different flavours and ingredients are used. The constant is dried broad beans, known as fava, or faba beans. The best are the skinless type: they cook quickly, taste better and have a more delicate texture.

italian bean dip

Soak the beans for 4 hours or overnight in cold water, or cheat by putting them in a saucepan, covering them with boiling water, bringing them to the boil and soaking for 2 hours with the heat turned off. Drain, then put them in a large saucepan with the bunch of herbs, onion and potato and add 2 litres boiling water. Bring to the boil and boil hard for 10 minutes. Reduce the heat and cook, part-covered for 1½–2 hours or until you can crush the beans easily with your thumbnail.

Drain the vegetables, reserving 2–3 tablespoons of cooking liquid. Discard the herbs. Working in batches if necessary, put the beans, potato, onion and garlic in a food processor, with the olive oil, lemon juice, oregano, salt and pepper. Blend in short bursts to a grainy but creamy purée.

Serve hot (as a side dish), warm or cool, sprinkled with extra olive oil. Serve as a dip or spread with baby leafy vegetables, radishes and cucumber or with toasted bread, or a combination.

Yoghurt in Greece is so rich, sharp and solid that it's almost like cheese, not yoghurt. If you can't find the real thing, you can strain plain yoghurt through muslin set in a sieve. You could also mix in cream cheese or even mash in a little feta cheese for stiffness. The finished dish should hold its shape. A dribble of greeny-gold Greek oil over the top is the final, and essential, detail.

tzatziki

250 g cucumber, unpeeled

2 teaspoons sea salt

3 garlic cloves, crushed

375 ml strained plain Greek yoghurt

4 tablespoons extra virgin olive oil

to serve (optional)

fresh mint leaves or parsley, chopped

black olives

bread

cucumber, cut in strips

carrots, cut in strips

serves 4–6: makes about 700 ml

Grate the cucumber coarsely, put it in a non-metal bowl, sprinkle with the salt, stir and let stand for 10 minutes. Put in a non-metal sieve and press hard to squeeze out the salt and liquid. Do not rinse. Return to a clean bowl and stir in the garlic and yoghurt.

Spoon into small individual serving dishes and drizzle with a little olive oil. Serve with chopped herbs, black olives, bread, cucumber and carrots.

Lemony, fresh hoummus and *hoummus bi tahini* (containing toasted sesame seed paste) are delicious Middle Eastern snack foods. The sesame richness has a more intense effect: but the simpler chickpea purée is also good. If possible, find dried chickpeas without skins (Greek grocers sometimes stock them). For 10-minute hoummus use canned chickpeas.

hoummus

If using dried chickpeas, put them in a bowl, cover with boiling water and leave for 3 hours (or in cold water for 8 hours). Drain. Put in a large saucepan, cover with boiling water, bring to the boil, part-cover and simmer for 1½–2½ hours or until the chickpeas are easily crushable and tender. Drain.

Put the chickpeas in a food processor with the lemon juice, garlic, ¼ teaspoon salt, pepper and the tahini paste, if using. Blend briefly to a mousse. With the machine running, pour the oil through the feed tube to form a creamy purée. Season to taste with salt and pepper.

Serve cool or chilled. You can also sprinkle a little hot red paprika on top and add the traditional trickle of extra virgin olive oil. Serve with crisp lettuce leaves and heated, torn or cut flatbreads and other crisp raw vegetables.

200 g dried chickpeas or 400 g cooked

freshly squeezed juice of 1 lemon

2 garlic cloves, crushed

2 tablespoons tahini paste (optional)

125 ml extra virgin olive oil

sea salt and freshly ground black pepper

to serve (optional)

hot paprika

extra virgin olive oil

lettuce leaves

flatbreads

crisp raw vegetables

serves 6–8: makes 400 ml

Beetroot hoummus is a delicious summery dip for vegetables or toasted bread. Cooking bread on the barbecue or a ridged stove-top grill pan is easy and very like the traditional way that pita bread is cooked.

beetroot hoummus
with pan-grilled bread

250 g cooked beetroot in natural juices, drained and chopped

25 g white breadcrumbs

1 garlic clove, crushed

3 tablespoons extra virgin olive oil

2 tablespoons hot horseradish sauce

1 tablespoon freshly squeezed lemon juice

sea salt and freshly ground black pepper

bread

250 g strong white flour, plus extra for kneading

1 teaspoon sea salt

1 teaspoon easy-blend dried yeast

1 tablespoon olive oil, plus extra for oiling the bowl

serves 6

To make the bread dough, sift the flour into the bowl of an electric mixer with the dough hook attached. Alternatively, use a food processor with the plastic blade attachment. Stir in the salt and yeast, then gradually work in 125 ml warm water and the oil to make a soft dough. Transfer to a lightly floured work surface and knead for 8–10 minutes until smooth and elastic.

Put the dough in an oiled bowl, cover with clingfilm and let rise in a warm place for 45 minutes or until doubled in size.

Meanwhile, to make the hoummus, put the beetroot, breadcrumbs, garlic oil, horseradish and lemon juice in a food processor, blend to a smooth purée and season with salt and pepper to taste.

Transfer the dough to a lightly floured work surface and knead it gently. Divide into 6 pieces and roll out each one to an oval, about the size of a pita bread. Cook the bread over medium-hot coals or on a preheated stove-top grill pan for 1–2 minutes on each side. Serve warm with the hoummus.

focaccia
with olives

This dough is a quick food processor version, which was originally developed for pizzas, but it makes excellent focaccia too. You could vary the recipe by using lemon instead of orange, and dried or fresh oregano instead of rosemary, plus other toppings such as anchovy-stuffed green olives.

1 sachet easy-blend dried yeast (7 g)

250 g plain white flour, plus 4 tablespoons for shaping

½ teaspoon sea salt flakes

2 tablespoons extra virgin olive oil, preferably Italian

topping

zest of 1 unwaxed orange, finely shredded, using a zester

grated zest and juice of 1 unwaxed orange

4 tablespoons extra virgin olive oil

2 garlic cloves, crushed

2 tablespoons fresh rosemary, coarsely chopped

½ teaspoon coarsely crushed black pepper

1 teaspoon sea salt flakes or crystals

150 g dry-cured black olives

a baking sheet, oiled

serves 4

Put the yeast, flour and salt in a food processor fitted with a plastic blade. Pulse briefly to sift the ingredients. Mix the oil with 180 ml warm water and, with the machine running, pour it all through the feed tube. Process, in short bursts, for 15 seconds until a soft mass forms (not a ball). It will be sticky and soft.

Scoop out the dough adding the extra 4 tablespoons flour as you knead, roll, pat and thump down the dough for 2 minutes on a work surface. Put the ball of dough in an oiled bowl. Enclose the whole bowl in a large plastic bag. Leave in a warm place until the dough has doubled in size, about 50 minutes.

Pat and stretch the dough into a rectangle about 32 x 22 cm. Transfer to an oiled baking sheet. Prod the dough all over with your fingertips to form dimples to take the topping.

Mix the orange zest and juice, oil, garlic, rosemary, pepper and half the salt in a bowl. Pour the mixture over the dough. Scatter with the olives, pushing them into the dimples. Let rest for 30 minutes.

Bake in a preheated oven at 200°C (400°F) Gas 6 for 25–30 minutes or until crusty and aromatic. Sprinkle with the remaining salt. Cut into generous squares, then serve hot or warm.

Hot from the grill, this aromatic herb bread is delicious used to mop up the wonderful meat juices from a barbecue, or eaten on its own with olive oil for dipping.

grilled rosemary flatbread

250 g strong white bread flour, plus extra for dusting

1½ teaspoons easy-blend dried yeast

1 teaspoon sea salt

1 tablespoon chopped fresh rosemary

120 ml hand-hot water

2 tablespoons extra virgin olive oil, plus extra for brushing

serves 4

Sift the flour into the bowl of an electric mixer and stir in the yeast, salt and rosemary. Add the hot water and olive oil and knead with the dough hook at high speed for about 8 minutes or until the dough is smooth and elastic. Alternatively, sift the flour into a large bowl and stir in the yeast, salt and rosemary. Make a well in the centre, then add the hot water and olive oil and mix to form a soft dough. Turn out onto a lightly floured work surface and knead until the dough is smooth and elastic.

Shape the dough into a ball, then put in an oiled bowl, cover with a tea towel and let rise in a warm place for 45–60 minutes or until doubled in size.

Punch down the dough and divide into 4 equal pieces. Roll each piece out on a lightly floured work surface to a 15 cm long oval.

Preheat the barbecue to low or wait until the coals are giving off a low heat. Brush the bread with a little olive oil and cook for 5 minutes, then brush the top with the remaining olive oil, flip and cook for a further 4–5 minutes until the bread is cooked through. Serve hot.

sweet things
& drinks

grilled figs
with almond mascarpone cream

150 g mascarpone cheese

½ teaspoon vanilla essence

*1 tablespoon toasted
ground almonds*

1 tablespoon Marsala wine

1 tablespoon clear honey

1 tablespoon caster sugar

*1 teaspoon ground
cardamom*

8–10 figs, halved

serves 4

This dish works well with stone fruits too,
such as plums, peaches or nectarines.

Put the mascarpone, vanilla essence, almonds,
Marsala wine and honey in a bowl and beat well.
Set aside in the refrigerator until required.

Put the sugar and ground cardamom in a
separate bowl and mix well, then carefully dip
the cut surface of the figs into the mixture.

Preheat the barbecue, then cook the figs over
medium-hot coals for 1–2 minutes on each side
until charred and softened.

Divide the grilled figs between 4 serving
bowls and serve with a dollop of the almond
mascarpone cream.

Wrapping fruits in foil is a great way to cook them on the barbecue – all the juices are contained in the parcel while the fruit softens.

grilled fruit parcels

4 peaches or nectarines, halved, stoned and sliced

200 g blueberries

125 g raspberries

freshly squeezed juice of 1 orange

1 teaspoon ground cinnamon

2 tablespoons caster sugar

200 g thick yoghurt

1 tablespoon clear honey

1 tablespoon rosewater

1 tablespoon chopped pistachio nuts

serves 4

Put the fruit in a large bowl, add the orange juice, cinnamon and sugar and mix well. Divide the fruit mixture among 4 sheets of foil. Fold the foil over the fruit and seal the edges to make parcels.

Put the yoghurt, honey and rosewater in a separate bowl and mix well. Set aside until required.

Preheat the barbecue, then cook the parcels over medium hot coals for 5–6 minutes. Remove the parcels from the heat, open carefully and transfer to 4 serving bowls. Serve with the yoghurt and a sprinkling of pistachio nuts.

Toasting the desiccated coconut enriches the ice cream and gives it a lovely nutty flavour. In this recipe it is served with wedges of barbecued pineapple, however, it works equally well with other fruits such as mango or peaches.

toasted coconut ice cream
with grilled pineapple

100 g soft brown sugar

100 g unsalted butter

100 ml dark rum

1 pineapple, medium or small, with leafy top if possible, cut lengthways into wedges and core removed

ice cream

25 g desiccated coconut

450 ml double cream

300 ml coconut milk

100 g caster sugar

5 egg yolks

an ice cream maker (optional)

serves 6

To make the ice cream, put the coconut in a dry frying pan and toast, stirring, over medium heat for 2–3 minutes until evenly browned. Transfer to a saucepan, then add the cream, coconut milk and sugar. Heat gently until it just reaches boiling point.

Put the egg yolks in a bowl and beat with a wooden spoon until pale. Stir about 2 tablespoons of the hot custard into the eggs, then return the mixture to the pan. Heat gently, stirring constantly until the mixture thickens enough to coat the back of the wooden spoon. Remove the pan from the heat and let cool completely.

When cold, strain the custard and freeze it in an ice cream maker according to the manufacturer's instructions. Transfer to the freezer. Alternatively, pour the cold custard in a plastic container and freeze for 5 hours, beating at hourly intervals with a balloon whisk.

Put the sugar, butter and rum in a small saucepan and heat until the sugar dissolves. Brush a little of the mixture over the pineapple wedges, then cook them on a preheated barbecue or on a stove-top grill pan for 2 minutes on each side until charred and tender. Serve with the ice cream and remaining rum sauce.

No one can resist these mixed fruit tarts – crumbling
pastry piled with fruits and served with whipped cream.

blue and red berry tarts

pastry

750 g plain flour

150 g unrefined caster sugar

525 g butter

6 egg yolks

filling

300 g blueberries

*250 g icing sugar, plus extra
for dusting*

1.2 litres double cream

*1 kg strawberries, hulled and
cut into bite-sized pieces*

500 g raspberries

300 g blackberries

3 loose-based tart tins,
23 cm diameter, buttered

greaseproof paper
and baking beans or
uncooked rice

serves 20

Put half the flour, half the sugar and half the butter in a food
processor and blend until the mixture looks like breadcrumbs.
Add 3 of the egg yolks and process again until the mixture forms
a ball. Remove and repeat with the remaining pastry ingredients.
Combine, then divide into 3 equal amounts. Wrap separately in
clingfilm and chill for about 20 minutes.

Transfer to a lightly floured work surface and roll out each pastry
portion until just larger than the tart tins. Line each tin with pastry,
prick the bases with a fork, then chill for 20 minutes.

Line the chilled pastry cases with greaseproof paper and baking
beans or rice. Cook in a preheated oven at 180°C (350°F) Gas 4
for 20 minutes. Remove the baking beans and paper, lower the
oven to 160°C (325°F) Gas 3 and cook the cases for 20 minutes
more until dry and golden. Remove from the oven and let cool.

Put the blueberries and half the icing sugar in a small saucepan.
Add 100 ml water and simmer gently for 5 minutes until the berries
are soft. Remove from the heat and let cool.

Put the cream in a bowl, add the remaining icing sugar and whisk
until soft peaks form. Add the strawberries, mix briefly, then spoon
into the cooled pastry cases. Pile the raspberries and blackberries
on top. Spoon over the stewed blueberries and remove the tarts
from the tins. Serve dusted with icing sugar.

Vanilla syrup transforms this cake into a lovely pudding, but you can also serve it simply with a spoonful of yoghurt.

lemon cake with vanilla syrup and strawberries

125 g unsalted butter, softened

125 g caster sugar

zest and juice of 2 unwaxed lemons

2 eggs, lightly beaten

200 g self-raising flour

50 g fine semolina

150 ml full-fat yoghurt

fresh strawberries, to serve

vanilla syrup

1 vanilla pod

150 g caster sugar

a springform cake tin, 23 cm diameter, greased and base-lined with baking parchment

serves 6

Put the butter, sugar and lemon zest in a bowl and whisk until pale and soft. Gradually beat in the eggs, a little at a time, until evenly mixed. Fold in the flour and semolina, then stir in the yoghurt and lemon juice.

Spoon the mixture into the prepared cake tin and bake in a preheated oven at 180°C (350°F) Gas 4 for about 40 minutes until risen and spongy. The cake is cooked when a skewer inserted into the centre of the cake comes out clean. Let cool in the tin for about 5 minutes, then turn out onto a wire rack to cool completely.

Meanwhile, to make the syrup, split the vanilla pod lengthways. Put the sugar and vanilla pod in a small saucepan and add 300 ml water. Heat gently until the sugar has dissolved. Bring to the boil and simmer for about 5 minutes until it becomes syrupy. Remove from the heat and let cool a little.

To serve, cut the cake into slices while still slightly warm, pour over the syrup and serve with strawberries.

A refreshing and summery sorbet – pretty and delicious when served with thin, crisp, almond biscuits. Roasting the plums before they are puréed will intensify their flavour.

caramelized plum sorbet

1 kg red plums, halved and pitted

2 tablespoons caster sugar

freshly squeezed juice of ½ lemon

sweet almond wafer biscuits, to serve (optional)

sugar syrup

300 ml sugar

1 vanilla pod, split lengthways

an ice cream maker (optional)

serves 6–8

Put the halved plums, cut side up, in a baking dish. Sprinkle with the sugar and bake in a preheated oven at 200°C (400°F) Gas 6 for 20 minutes until golden and softened. Remove from the oven and let cool completely.

Transfer the plums to a blender and purée until very smooth. Stir in the lemon juice.

Meanwhile, to make the sugar syrup, put the sugar and vanilla pod in a saucepan, add 600 ml water and heat gently until the sugar has dissolved. Bring to the boil, then reduce the heat and simmer for 5 minutes. Let cool, remove the vanilla pod, then stir the syrup into the plum purée.

Transfer the mixture to an ice cream maker and churn, according to the manufacturer's instructions. Store in the freezer until required.

Alternatively, transfer the purée to a plastic container and freeze for 5 hours, beating at hourly intervals with a balloon whisk. (This will break down the ice crystals and make the sorbet smooth.) Serve with the almond biscuits, if using.

A wonderfully indulgent and nostalgic English sundae, based on an American classic – even more amazing than the original.

knickerbocker glory

2 scoops vanilla ice cream

about 3–4 tablespoons fresh raspberries, crushed with a fork

1 scoop strawberry ice cream

1–2 tablespoons chopped fresh fruit, such as pineapple or apricots

about 1–2 tablespoons whipped cream

about 1 teaspoon toasted slivered almonds, coarsely crushed

1 glacé cherry

hot chocolate sauce

155 g bitter chocolate (70 per cent cocoa solids)

250 ml double cream

4 tablespoons sugar

a tall soda glass

serves 1

To make the chocolate sauce, melt the chocolate in a bowl set over a saucepan of simmering water – don't let the water touch the bowl. Put the cream and sugar in a saucepan and heat until almost boiling. Stir the hot cream mixture into the chocolate and mix well.

Carefully spoon about 2 tablespoons of the chocolate sauce into the bottom of a tall soda glass. Add 2 scoops vanilla ice cream, then the crushed fresh raspberries.

Add 1 scoop strawberry ice cream, then a layer of chopped fresh pineapple or apricots. Top with a big cloud of whipped cream and sprinkle with toasted almonds and a cherry.

Put a parfait spoon into the glass and serve.

Hot sauces make a delicious contrast with cold ice cream. This one is butterscotch, but try Hot Fudge Sauce (page 204) if you prefer.

hot butterscotch sundae

To make the nut brittle, put 6 tablespoons water and the sugar in a saucepan, stir well, then bring to the boil over medium heat. Continue boiling until golden brown. Stir in the nuts, pour onto the prepared baking sheet, then let cool and set. When set, break up the brittle, then crush with a rolling pin.

To make the butterscotch sauce, put the sugar, cream and butter in a saucepan and stir over medium heat until melted and boiling. Reduce the heat and simmer for 3 minutes.

Put 3 scoops chocolate or vanilla ice cream in the base of each sundae dish and balance 1 scoop coffee or vanilla ice cream on top. Spoon 2 tablespoons hot butterscotch sauce around the ice cream in each dish, then pour 2 tablespoons sauce over the top. Sprinkle with nut brittle and serve.

12 scoops very cold chocolate or vanilla ice cream

4 scoops very cold coffee or vanilla ice cream

nut brittle

75 g sugar

50 g pecans or almonds, coarsely crushed

butterscotch sauce

100 g soft brown sugar

125 ml double cream

5 tablespoons butter

1 baking sheet, greased

4 metal sundae dishes or thick, heatproof glass bowls

serves 4

Fudge – whether hot or cold – is one of the great soda fountain classics. Pour hot fudge sauce over this indulgent combination of fruit and ice cream for a real summertime treat.

fudge sauce sundae

12 scoops very cold vanilla ice cream

4 apricots, fresh or canned, sliced (optional)

12 tablespoons stiffly whipped cream

4 fan-shaped wafers

pineapple syrup

1 large ripe pineapple, peeled and core removed

sugar (see method)

strawberry sauce

3 punnets strawberries

1 tablespoon freshly squeezed lemon juice

4 tablespoons sugar

hot fudge sauce

100 g dark chocolate, chopped

30 g unsalted butter

100 g dark brown sugar

2 tablespoons golden syrup

125 ml double cream

4 heatproof sundae glasses

serves 4

To make the pineapple syrup, cut the pineapple flesh into chunks and put in a food processor or blender. Blend until smooth, then add 100 g sugar for every 150 ml pulp. Blend again. Transfer to a stainless steel saucepan, bring slowly to the boil, reduce the heat, then simmer for about 10 minutes, stirring frequently. Let cool, then chill.

To make the strawberry sauce, put the strawberries, lemon juice and sugar in a saucepan and heat gently until the juices run. When the berries have become pale and the juice dark, press through a plastic sieve or simply strain the juice. Let cool.

To make the fudge sauce, put the chocolate, butter, sugar, golden syrup and cream in a saucepan and heat, stirring, until melted. Bring to the boil, then remove from the heat.

Put 1 scoop vanilla ice cream in a sundae glass, then add 1 tablespoon pineapple syrup and 1 sliced apricot, if using. Add 3 tablespoons whipped cream, then 2 tablespoons strawberry sauce. Add 2 more scoops ice cream, then spoon 2–3 tablespoons hot fudge sauce over the top. Repeat to make 4 sundaes. Serve topped with a wafer.

s'mores

This is one for the kids. S'mores are an American campfire classic where graham crackers, barbecued marshmallows and chocolate squares are sandwiched together making a delicious, gooey taste sensation. You can use a sweet biscuit, such as langue du chat or almond thins instead of graham crackers, but any will do.

16 biscuits, such as digestive biscuits or almond thins

8 pieces of plain chocolate

16 marshmallows

8 metal skewers

serves 4

Put half the biscuits on a plate and top each one with a square of chocolate.

Preheat the barbecue. Thread 2 marshmallows onto each skewer and cook over hot coals for about 2 minutes, turning constantly until the marshmallows are melted and blackened. Remove from the heat and let cool slightly.

Put the marshmallows onto the chocolate squares and sandwich together with the remaining biscuits. Gently ease out the skewers and serve the s'mores as soon as the chocolate melts.

Whenever you squeeze fruit juice, pour some into ice cube trays and freeze for later.

fruit frappé

500 ml freshly squeezed fruit juice, such as apple, raspberry, pineapple

serves 2

Freeze the juice in ice cube trays. When ready to serve, transfer to a food processor and zap in short bursts until crushed but not slushy.

Alternatively, put the ice cubes in the refrigerator for a couple of minutes to soften a little, then mash them with a fork.

Serve in chilled glasses.

Iced coffee can be surprisingly refreshing on a hot day. To make this extra special, add a tablespoon of rum or brandy.

iced coffee

125 ml strong espresso coffee, cooled and chilled

250 ml milk or cream

1 scoop vanilla ice cream

to serve

1–2 tablespoons whipped cream

1 coffee bean, crushed (optional)

sugar, to taste

serves 1

Put the coffee in a blender with the milk or cream and ice cream and blend until smooth. Pour into a glass and top with a swirl of whipped cream and a sprinkling of crushed coffee bean, if using. Serve sugar separately and sweeten to taste.

variation Make the iced coffee as in the main recipe, stir in 1 tablespoon rum or brandy and top with whipped cream.

strawberry, pear and orange frappé

400 g strawberries, hulled

4 pears, quartered and cored

300 ml freshly squeezed orange juice

ice cubes, to serve (optional)

serves 4

For this fresh juice you really need a juicer, but at a pinch you could purée the fruits in a blender. Always make fresh juices just before serving, because they can discolour and separate quickly.

Push the strawberries and pears through a juicer and transfer to a jug. Add the orange juice, stir to mix, then pour into glasses half filled with ice cubes, if using. Serve at once.

ginger and lime cordial

150 g fresh ginger

2 unwaxed limes, sliced

500 g granulated sugar

to serve

ice cubes

unwaxed lime wedges

sparkling water

1 sterilized bottle, 750 ml (page 4)

makes about 750 ml

A lovely refreshing cordial with a delicious kick of ginger – perfect for any occasion.

Using a sharp knife, peel and thinly slice the ginger, then pound lightly with a rolling pin. Put it in a saucepan, add the lime slices and 1 litre water, bring to the boil, part-cover with a lid and simmer gently for 45 minutes. Remove from the heat, add the sugar and stir until dissolved. Let cool, strain and pour the cordial into a sterilized bottle. Seal and store until ready to use.

When ready to serve, pour a little cordial into a glass, add ice cubes and lime wedges and top up with sparkling water.

strawberry and banana ice cream shake

250 g ripe strawberries, hulled

1 ripe banana, peeled and chopped

4 scoops strawberry ice cream, plus extra to serve (optional)

200 ml milk

serves 3–4

A great shake for when you're in serious ice cream mode. Also, try mango and banana with vanilla ice cream.

Put the strawberries, banana, ice cream and milk in a blender and purée until very smooth. Pour into glasses and serve topped with extra ice cream, if using.

vanilla milkshake

250 ml milk

2 teaspoons sugar or sugar syrup*

a drop of vanilla essence

1 scoop vanilla ice cream

125 ml crushed ice (optional)

serves 1

*To make sugar syrup, put 1 part sugar to 3 parts water in a saucepan and heat gently until the sugar dissolves and the mixture becomes a light syrup.

You can buy drink mixer machines based on the old soda fountain classics – or use a blender instead. Crushed ice will make the drink froth more.

Put all the ingredients in a blender (with the ice) or drink mixer and blend until frothy. Transfer to a metal milkshake container and serve separately with a saucer, napkins and a tall soda glass, plus straws and a parfait spoon.

variation Instead of the sugar syrup and vanilla, use 1 tablespoon Hot Chocolate Sauce (page 200).

champagne cocktails

There is something decidedly decadent about
a glass of fizz in the morning, so if you're going
to treat yourself to brunch, why not totally spoil
yourself with one of these cocktails.

campari fizz

6 shots of Campari

3 teaspoons caster sugar

*1 bottle chilled sparkling wine,
750 ml*

serves 6

Pour the Campari into
6 champagne flutes and
sweeten each one with
½ teaspoon sugar. Top up
with sparkling wine and serve.

peach bellini

3 ripe peaches

*1 bottle chilled Prosecco
or sparkling wine, 750 ml*

serves 6

Peel the peaches by
plunging them into boiling
water for 30 seconds.
Refresh them under cold
water and peel off the skin.
Cut in half, remove the stone
and chop the flesh.

Put the peaches in a blender,
add a small amount of
Prosecco and process to
a purée. Divide between
6 champagne flutes, top up
with the remaining Prosecco
and serve.

mimosa

*6 blood oranges or regular
oranges*

*1 bottle chilled sparkling wine,
750 ml*

serves 6

Squeeze the oranges and
divide the juice among
6 glasses. Top up with
sparkling wine and serve.

217 sweet things & drinks

This is a pretty spritzer to cool a hot brow on a sunny day. The frozen grapes act as original ice cubes, keeping the wine chilled and also make it look amazing.

white wine spritzer

1 bottle white wine, 750 ml, chilled

1 litre sparkling mineral water, chilled

400 g white grapes, frozen

serves 8

Put the chilled white wine, mineral water and frozen grapes in a large jug and mix well. Serve the spritzer in your favourite large glasses.

variation Frozen fruit cubes are great to take on picnics to chill drinks. They do not melt as quickly as ordinary ice cubes and children love eating them too. Try chopping up some orange segments, putting them in ice cube trays, covering with fresh orange juice, then freezing.

*4 shots iced vodka,
preferably Absolut*

4 shots lime cordial

*a few drops of
Angostura bitters*

to serve

ice cubes

1 unwaxed lemon, sliced

tonic water

serves 4

Vodka and lime is a classic combination and here the drink is given a refreshing twist with the addition of a few drops of Angostura bitters.

iced long vodka

Pour the vodka, lime cordial and a little Angostura bitters into 4 tall glasses and add ice cubes and lemon slices. Top up with tonic water and serve.

fruit and herb pimm's

A balmy summer's evening seems the perfect time for a glass of Pimm's overflowing with soft fruits and fresh herbs. You can vary the fruits as you wish, but always include some slices of cucumber and a handful of fresh mint leaves.

Pour the Pimm's into a large jug and add the halved strawberries, chopped melon or nectarine slices, lemon slices, cucumber slices and some mint and borage flowers, if using. Set aside to infuse for 30 minutes. Pour into tall glasses filled with ice cubes and top up with lemonade or ginger ale.

1 bottle Pimm's No 1

*250 g strawberries, hulled
and halved*

*½ melon, deseeded and
chopped, or nectarine slices*

1 unwaxed lemon, sliced

½ cucumber, sliced

a few fresh mint leaves

*a few fresh borage flowers
(optional)*

to serve

ice cubes

*1 bottle lemonade or
ginger ale*

serves 12

This tastes and looks heavenly, but has the effect of dynamite! If you can't get seedless watermelon, just use a regular one and deseed it.

vodka watermelon

1 seedless watermelon, chilled

1 bottle chilled vodka, 750 ml

to serve

lime wedges

ice cubes

serves 20

Cut the melon in half and scoop out all the flesh. Put it in a blender and process until smooth. Remove to a large jug, add the vodka and let chill for 2 hours before serving. Serve with lime wedges and ice.

variation Replace the vodka with sparkling water or lemonade, for those with a sweet tooth.

lemonade
with mint and bitters

1 litre lemonade

6 sprigs of mint

Angostura bitters

lemon slices

ice cubes

serves 6

A delightfully simple drink, ideal for hot summer days. The bitters give the lemonade a refreshing, herbal flavour and make it a pretty pale pink.

Pour the lemonade into 6 tall glasses. Add a sprig of mint, a few drops of bitters, a few slices of lemon and ice cubes to each one, then serve at once.

stick drinks

You can use almost any fruit in a stick drink, as long as you include chopped limes and sugar.

lime and mint stick drink

12 large fresh mint leaves
2 teaspoons brown sugar
1 lime, finely diced, including zest
ice cubes
2 large shots Bacardi rum
soda water

cocktail shaker or jug
2 cocktail glasses

serves 2

Put the mint leaves, sugar and lime in a shaker or jug and mash with a stick or spoon until quite pulpy. Alternatively, use a mortar and pestle.

Fill 2 glasses with ice to chill them thoroughly, then tip the ice into the mashed mint mixture. Add the Bacardi to the mixture, shake well, then pour back into the glasses. Add a little soda water and serve.

kiwi fruit, passionfruit and lime sticky

1 large lime, diced
1 large kiwi fruit, peeled and diced
12 fresh mint leaves
1 tablespoon caster sugar
1 large passionfruit, halved
ice cubes
2 large shots vodka

cocktail shaker or jug
2 cocktail glasses

serves 2

Put the lime and kiwi fruit in a shaker or jug, add the mint, sugar and passionfruit pulp and seeds. Mash well until pulpy.

Fill 2 glasses with ice to chill them thoroughly, then tip the ice into the kiwi fruit mixture. Add the vodka, shake or stir well, then pour back into the glasses. Serve at once.

basics

Vinaigrette can be a simple thing – just oil, vinegar or other acidulator such as citrus juice, plus salt and freshly ground black pepper. You can add lots of other things to ring the changes, see the variations given below. Use the best oil you can find, and use as little vinegar as possible.

vinaigrette

6 tablespoons extra virgin olive oil

1 tablespoon white wine vinegar

sea salt and freshly ground black pepper

makes about 125 ml

Put the oil, vinegar, salt and pepper in a salad bowl and beat with a fork or small whisk.

variations   Add 1 teaspoon Dijon mustard and beat well. The mustard helps form an emulsion.

Use harissa paste instead of mustard.

Use Japanese rice vinegar, which gives a mild, smooth taste, instead of white wine vinegar. You can also substitute red wine vinegar, sherry vinegar, cider vinegar, or others.

Use freshly squeezed lime or lemon juice instead of vinegar.

Instead of extra virgin, use 2 tablespoons mild virgin olive oil and 3 tablespoons nut oil such as walnut, hazelnut or macadamia. Nut oils turn rancid very quickly, so buy small quantities, keep in the refrigerator and use quickly.

Heat the vinaigrette in a small saucepan over gentle heat until just warm, then pour over the salad.

pesto

Although in Italy pesto is only served with pasta, the rest of the world has fallen in love with it. It makes a delicious dressing for many kinds of salad – potato, tomato, chickpeas and beans – or stirred through rice or couscous with extra herbs.

basil pesto

4 tablespoons pine nuts
4 garlic cloves, crushed
1 teaspoon sea salt
a large double handful of fresh basil leaves
25 g freshly grated Parmesan cheese
125 ml extra virgin olive oil, or to taste

makes about 250 ml

Put the pine nuts in a dry frying pan and fry gently and quickly until golden (about 30 seconds). They burn very easily, so don't leave them. Let cool. Transfer to a food processor or blender, add the garlic, salt and basil and purée to a paste. Add the Parmesan, blend again, then add the oil and blend again until smooth. Add extra oil if you want a looser texture.

red pesto

Instead of basil, use 250 g sun-dried tomatoes bottled in olive oil, but drained. A teaspoon of harissa paste lifts the flavour even further.

parsley pesto

Make a much milder version using parsley instead of basil when the basil has not yet reached its full summer flavour, or all you have is the infant supermarket kind. Try almonds instead of pine nuts in this pesto.

rocket pesto

Use half parsley and half rocket leaves instead of the basil.

250 g white cabbage, thinly sliced

175 g carrots, grated

½ white onion, thinly sliced

2 teaspoons caster sugar

1 tablespoon white wine vinegar

50 g Mayonnaise (below)

2 tablespoons double cream

1 tablespoon wholegrain mustard

sea salt and freshly ground black pepper

serves 4

Home-made coleslaw is a million miles away from the shop-bought version. It's well worth the effort.

creamy coleslaw

Put the cabbage, carrots and onion in a colander and sprinkle with 1 teaspoon salt, the sugar and vinegar. Stir well and let drain over a bowl for 30 minutes.

Squeeze out excess liquid from the vegetables and put them in a large bowl. Put the mayonnaise, cream and mustard in a separate bowl and mix well, then stir into the cabbage mixture. Season to taste with salt and pepper and serve. Store in the refrigerator for up to 3 days.

mayonnaise

Don't use an extra virgin olive oil, otherwise the sauce can become slightly bitter.

2 egg yolks

2 teaspoons white wine vinegar or freshly squeezed lemon juice

2 teaspoons Dijon mustard

300 ml olive oil

sea salt and freshly ground black pepper

makes about 300 ml

Put the egg yolks, vinegar, mustard and ¼ teaspoon salt in a food processor and blend briefly until frothy. With the machine running, gradually pour in the olive oil in a slow steady stream until all the oil is incorporated and the sauce is thick and glossy.

If the sauce is too thick, add 1–2 tablespoons boiling water and blend again briefly. Season to taste with salt and pepper, then cover the surface of the mayonnaise with clingfilm. Store in the refrigerator for up to 3 days.

sauces

barbecue sauce

200 ml tomato passata

100 ml maple syrup

50 ml dark treacle

50 ml tomato ketchup

50 ml white wine vinegar

3 tablespoons Worcestershire sauce

1 tablespoon Dijon mustard

1 teaspoon garlic powder

1/4 teaspoon hot paprika

sea salt and freshly ground black pepper

makes about 400 ml

Put all the ingredients in a small saucepan, bring to the boil and simmer gently for 10–15 minutes until reduced slightly and thickened. Season to taste with salt and pepper and let cool.

Pour into an airtight container and store in the refrigerator for up to 2 weeks.

asian barbecue sauce

100 ml tomato passata

50 ml hoisin sauce

1 teaspoon hot chilli sauce

2 garlic cloves, crushed

2 tablespoons sweet soy sauce

1 tablespoon rice wine vinegar

1 teaspoon ground coriander

1/2 teaspoon ground cinnamon

1/4 teaspoon Chinese five-spice powder

makes about 350 ml

Put all the ingredients in a small saucepan, add 100 ml water, bring to the boil and simmer gently for 10 minutes. Remove from the heat and let cool.

Pour into an airtight container and store in the refrigerator for up to 2 weeks.

note The recipe for Reduced Balsamic Vinegar (far right) is given on page 147.

sweet chilli sauce

6 large red chillies, deseeded and chopped

4 garlic cloves, chopped

1 teaspoon grated fresh ginger

1 teaspoon sea salt

100 ml rice wine vinegar

100 ml sugar

makes about 200 ml

Put the chillies, garlic, ginger and salt in a food processor and blend to a coarse paste. Transfer to a saucepan, add the vinegar and sugar, bring to the boil and simmer gently, part-covered, for 5 minutes until the mixture becomes a thin syrup. Remove from the heat and let cool.

Pour into an airtight container and store in the refrigerator for up to 2 weeks.

marinades

thai spice

2 stalks of lemongrass

6 kaffir lime leaves

2 garlic cloves, coarsely chopped

2 cm fresh ginger, coarsely chopped

4 coriander roots, washed and dried

2 small fresh red chillies, deseeded
and coarsely chopped

200 ml extra virgin olive oil

2 tablespoons sesame oil

2 tablespoons Thai fish sauce

makes about 300 ml

Using a sharp knife, trim the lemongrass stalk to 15 cm, then remove and discard the tough outer layers. Chop the inner stalk.

Pound the lemongrass stalks, lime leaves, garlic, ginger, coriander roots and chillies with a pestle to release the aromas.

Put the mixture in a bowl, add the oils and fish sauce and set aside to infuse until ready to use.

minted yoghurt

2 teaspoons coriander seeds

1 teaspoon cumin seeds

250 ml thick yoghurt

freshly squeezed juice of ½ lemon

1 tablespoon extra virgin olive oil

1 teaspoon grated fresh ginger

½ teaspoon sea salt

2 garlic cloves, crushed

2 tablespoons chopped fresh
mint leaves

¼ teaspoon chilli powder

makes about 275 ml

Put the spices in a dry frying pan and toast over medium heat until golden and aromatic. Remove from the heat and let cool. Transfer to a spice grinder (or clean coffee grinder) and crush to a coarse powder.

Put the spices in a bowl, add the yoghurt, lemon juice, oil, ginger, salt, garlic, mint and chilli powder. Mix well. Set aside to infuse until ready to use.

herb, lemon and garlic

2 sprigs of rosemary

2 sprigs of thyme

4 bay leaves

2 large garlic cloves, coarsely chopped

pared zest of 1 unwaxed lemon

1 teaspoon black peppercorns,
coarsely crushed

200 ml extra virgin olive oil

makes about 300 ml

Strip the rosemary and thyme leaves from the stalks and put them in a mortar. Add the bay leaves, garlic and lemon zest and pound with a pestle to release the aromas.

Transfer the mixture to a bowl, stir in the peppercorns and olive oil and set aside to infuse until ready to use.

index

credits

Photographs

Ian Wallace Back endpapers right, pages 3 background, inset left & inset centre right, 6 right, 6–7, 9 inset centre left & right, 13, 14, 17, 34, 35 inset left & inset centre right, 58, 61, 63 inset centre right, 66, 73, 77, 78, 81 inset centre left, 82, 92, 93 background, insets left & centre right, 95, 103, 108, 111, 115 inset centre left, 120, 128, 135, 136 insets left, centre left & right, 141–150, 153, 154, 157, 161–173, 175 insets left & centre left, 181, 185, 187 background, inset centre left & centre right, 189, 190, 193, 198, 199, 206, 211, 212, 215, 219, 221, 223, 225 insets right & centre left, 230, 233, 234

Debi Treloar Pages 1, 2, 3 inset centre left & inset right, 4, 5, 63 background & inset left, 69, 70, 74, 81 inset centre right, 85, 86, 107, 139 inset centre right, 158, 174, 175 background, 186, 187 inset left, 194, 201–205, 208, 209, 216, 220

Peter Cassidy Pages 10, 16, 21, 25, 29, 30, 33, 35 inset right, 37–57, 65, 81 inset left, 89, 90, 96, 100, 116, 124, 178, 179, 182, 225 insets left & centre right, 226, 229, 238

Martin Brigdale Pages 22, 93 insets right & centre left, 104, 112, 115 insets left, centre right & right, 119, 131, 132, 136, 175 inset centre right, 176

William Lingwood Pages 26, 31, 67, 99, 101, 106, 123, 126–127, 133, 151, 180, 228

Jan Baldwin Pages 8, 9 inset left & centre right, 35 background & inset centre left, 115 background, 225 background

Christopher Drake Back endpapers left, pages 62, 63 insets right & centre left, 138, 187 inset right

Pia Tryde Front endpapers right, pages 81 background & inset right, 114

Nicky Dowey Pages 23, 36, 60, 237

Chris Tubbs Front endpapers left, pages 9 background, 80, 240

Gus Filgate Pages 18, 175 inset right

David Brittain Pages 6 left, 224

Caroline Arber Page 87

Polly Wreford Page 139 background

Francesca Yorke Page 214

Recipes

LOUISE PICKFORD

Barbecued fish bathed in oregano and lemon
Barbecued Mexican-style poussins
Beetroot hoummus with pan-grilled bread
Butterflied lamb with white bean salad
Caramelized plum sorbet
Champagne cocktails
Charred leeks with tarator sauce
Chicken caesar wraps
Chicken lemon skewers
Chicken panini with roasted pepper and rocket aïoli
Chicken salad with radicchio and pine nuts
Chicken skewers with sesame and thyme
Chilled coconut soup with sizzling prawns
Chilli tuna tartare pasta
Clam parcels with garlic butter
Coleslaw
Fragrant herb couscous salad
Fresh pea and lettuce risotto
Fruit and herb pimm's
Ginger and lime cordial
Grilled corn with chilli salt rub
Grilled figs with almond mascarpone cream
Grilled fruit parcels
Grilled miso cod
Grilled rosemary flatbread
Iced long vodka
Jerk chicken wings with avocado salsa
Lamb burgers with mint yoghurt
Lamb kebabs with warm chickpea salad
Lemonade with mint and bitters
Lemon cake with vanilla syrup and strawberries
Marinades
Mayonnaise
Mixed mushroom frittata
Orange and soy glazed duck
Orzo salad with lemon and herb dressing
Pappa al pomodoro
Pasta with fresh tomato
Prawn, chorizo and sage skewers
Rib eye steaks with anchovy butter

Sage-rubbed pork chops
Salt-crusted prawns with tomato, avocado and olive salad
Sauces
Scallops with lemongrass and lime butter
Seared squid with lemon and coriander dressing
Seared swordfish with new potatoes, beans and olives
Simple tomato and olive tart
Slow-roasted tomatoes with ricotta and spaghetti
S'Mores
Stick drinks
Strawberry and banana ice cream shake
Strawberry, pear and orange frappé
Summer vegetables with bagna cauda
Sweetcorn griddle cakes
Tex-mex pork rack
Thai-style beef salad
Tiger prawns with herb mayonnaise
Toasted coconut ice cream with grilled pineapple
Turkish pizza turnover
Vegetable antipasto
Whole salmon stuffed with herbs

ELSA PETERSEN-SCHEPELERN

Avocado salad
Caesar salad
Fruit frappé
Fudge sauce sundae
Greek salad
Hot butterscotch sundae
Iced coffee
Italian grilled pepper salad
Knickerbocker glory
Pesto
Quick chickpea salad
Salade Niçoise
Tonno e fagioli
Tuscan panzanella
Vanilla milkshake
Vinaigrette

CLARE FERGUSON

Antipodean potato salad
Asparagus with prosciutto
Focaccia with olives

Greek chicken stifado
Hoummus
Italian bean dip
Marinated black olives
Mozzarella, tomato and rocket salad
Paella
Pappardelle with basil oil
Pizza napoletana
Radicchio with gorgonzola and walnuts
Souvlaki in pita
Spanish tart with peppers
Tzatziki

FRAN WARDE

Baked aubergines with pesto sauce
Blue and red berry tarts
Chicken and tarragon pesto pasta
Mozzarella baked tomatoes
Rosemary and lemon roasted chicken
Summer salad
Toasted ciabatta pizzas
Vodka watermelon
White wine spritzer

JULZ BERESFORD

Chorizo in red wine
Fried squid Roman-style
Gazpacho
Marinated anchovies

MAXINE CLARK

Cherry tomato, bocconcini and basil bruschetta
Salmon frittata with potatoes and asparagus
Salmon in lemon cream sauce with dill tagliatelle
Smoked and fresh salmon terrine

SILVANA FRANCO

Seafood spaghettini

LESLEY WATERS

Courgette quiche with sun-dried tomatoes